Founding Mothers

Linda Grant De Pauw

Founding Mothers

Women in America in the Revolutionary Era

Wood Engravings by Michael McCurdy

HOUGHTON MIFFLIN COMPANY BOSTON

Library of Congress Cataloging in Publication Data

De Pauw, Linda Grant.
  Founding mothers: women of America in the Revolutionary era.

  SUMMARY: Describes the daily lives, social roles, and contributions of women living
during the revolutionary period. 1. Women — United States — History —Juvenile literature. 2. Women — United States — Social conditions — Juvenile literature. 3. Women's
rights — United States — History. 4. United States — Social life and customs — Colonial
period, ca. 1600-1775 — Juvenile literature. [1. Women — History. 2. Women — Social conditions.
3. United States — Social life and customs — Colonial period, ca. 1600-1775]   I. Title.
HQ1416.D46   301.41'2'0973   75-17031
HC ISBN 0-395-21896-9   PA ISBN 0-395-70109-0

For Jolie and Benjamin

CONTENTS

INTRODUCTION

WHEN our school books tell us of the birth of the United States they emphasize the activities of the "founding fathers." These founders, they tell us, were the handful of wealthy, educated, white males who wrote the Declaration of Independence in 1776 and the Constitution of the United States in 1787. The American way of life, however, did not spring from these bits of parchment, although we are rightly proud of these documents. They express the principles of justice, humanity, and equality that have served as our national ideals for almost two hundred years. They still inspire us today as we continue to try to extend the "inalienable rights of man"

to people of all races, to children, and to women. The
men who wrote the Declaration of Independence and the
Constitution did not, however, invent the ideals these
documents embody nor did they make them operative.
The real founders of the United States were not the small
number of "founding fathers" but the two and a half
million people who lived in the eastern part of North
America and who made up our founding generation. It is
obvious that without these ordinary people the nation we
know today would not have been born. Only occasionally do our school books give us a glimpse of some of
these ordinary people. We read about the common
soldiers freezing at Valley Forge, of the black man
Crispus Attucks who fell during the Boston Massacre,
and of Indian warriors who fought on both sides during
the war for American independence. Such men should
certainly be remembered along with the statesmen and
generals. Even more hidden than the ordinary men of the
Revolutionary generation are the women who lived
through those historic years.

Almost half of the Revolutionary generation was
female. Fine ladies, servant girls, black slave women,
middle-class matrons, and native American women all
contributed to the development of American life. They
may be invisible in history books but they were present
everywhere that men were. They were on farms
and plantations, in the cities and in the forests. They ran
businesses, served with the armies, and participated in

political decision-making. The sex stereotypes and legal restrictions that so severely hampered women's activities in the nineteenth century were relatively weak in the eighteenth. Consequently women participated in the social, economic, political, and military activities of the day in ways that would be thought highly improper if not impossible for women a generation later.

Until very recently the writers of history books did not think the activities of women were worth recording. They did not think anyone would be interested in reading about the lives of ordinary people, especially not ordinary women. One basic principle of the American Revolution, however, was the conviction that ordinary people are just as important as kings and governors and generals. Many historians today are beginning to believe they are even more interesting. This book, then, is about the hidden heroines of the Revolutionary generation — women whose lives, whether dramatic or routine, were an essential part of our history. These are the "founding mothers."

1

WOMEN'S WORK: MAKING A HOME

Homemaking in preindustrial America required both strength and skill. Marriages were not viewed primarily as romantic alliances but as economic partnerships that enabled the individuals involved to set up households of their own. Those who were too poor to marry had to live all their lives in someone else's household — that of a parent, relative, or master. Those who set up independent households could not only raise a family of children but could also take in servants and apprentices. Controlling the labor of so many people, the householder could accumulate property. Property, in turn, meant social status, and, for the husband, political rights. Thus men and women who contracted a marriage were expected to have the training and skills that would allow them to run a household that would not merely provide comfort but would also produce a profit.

Merely providing comfort, however, required proficiency in many skills that were essential in an age when the basic needs of life could not be purchased in supermarkets or department stores. It is difficult for us to appreciate how few items in a typical eighteenth-century home were purchased from outside. Salt, tea, and metal items such as kettles, knives, needles, and nails, had to come from a shop. Most other items were produced at home or from the household manufacture of a neighbor and were paid for from the profit of one's own domestic industry. Frugality and self-sufficiency ranked high among colonial virtues.

Men as well as women had "homemaking" duties in the eighteenth century. Men built the homes and made the furniture. They cleared the land, built fences, plowed the fields, and raised the grain for the family's table and perhaps a bit of tobacco or other cash crop. Slaughtering the larger domestic animals was also "man's work" as was hunting and fishing. If the family owned a shop or other business, the husband usually ran it.

Women who were widowed or whose husbands were ill or away from home for long periods might do all of the "man's work" as well as their own. But there was so much work in a colonial household that some division of labor was a necessity. "Woman's work" included five main areas of responsibility: feeding the family; manufacturing the family's clothing and such household essentials as candles and soap; keeping the home, the family, and the family's clothing clean; serving as doctor, nurse, and midwife for all members of the household including servants and slaves; and caring for children, both the mother's own and apprentices or children of relatives who lived with the family. All of these tasks were done by the mistress of the household herself or delegated to a child, slave, or servant under the mistress's careful supervision.

Feeding the family began with maintaining a fire for cooking. Fuel must be brought into the house and the fire be constantly fed and carefully banked at night. In the winter, when the temperature might fall below freezing even a few feet from the fire, it was no doubt a comfort to sit close to the fireplace. But the fire had to be maintained just as carefully in summer, for there were no matches and rekindling a dead fire was a serious undertaking. Consequently, women continued to tend the fire even in the hottest days of August, for there were few foods in the colonial diet that could be eaten raw.

Tending the kitchen garden was a second basic chore. Although the staple grain and the cash crop were grown in fields tended by the men, vegetables for the table and the herbs needed for medicines came from plots tended by women. The men plowed the kitchen garden in the spring, but the rest of the work from planting to harvesting was done by women. The crops grown in the kitchen gardens varied in different parts of the country. Root plants, which could be stored for winter consumption, were more popular than salad greens. Potatoes, carrots, turnips, and beets were common as were a variety of beans. Kitchen gardens might be large or small depending upon the number of people in the household and the family's wealth. But every woman had one, and even in town plots of vegetables and herbs were cultivated.

In addition to tending the garden, colonial women were responsible for the barnyard animals. Preparation of a chicken stew began with the cook catching, slaughtering, cleaning, and plucking the chicken. Pigs were the most common barnyard animal because they could easily forage their own food in the woods. Women turned them into bacon, ham, sausages, and salt pork.

The creativity of colonial women rarely went into planning their menus. Colonial families did not expect their meals to be "interesting" or to have something different to eat for dinner every day. Women prepared the same dishes for weeks on end — or even months on end during the winter — feeding the family what was available. Only the very wealthy had a surplus of food and a large number of servants that made lavish dining in the manner of the European aristocracy possible. For most Americans the typical meal — breakfast, lunch, or dinner — included salt meat or fish, corn cakes of some sort, and whiskey or rum with water. These items were the colonial American equivalent of our hamburger, French fries, and 'shake.

Cooking was done in the ashes of the fire, in ovens built into the side of the fireplace, or in large kettles made of iron, brass, or copper. Since a typical household included many people, these kettles frequently weighed between forty and seventy pounds empty and held as much as fifteen gallons of soup or stew. The kettle was held over the fire by an iron crane or it might stand on its own legs over the coals. Obviously, the manipulation of any of this apparatus over the hot flames took considerable muscle power.

A colonial family's protein came in different forms in different parts of the country. Wild game — deer, moose, bear, rabbit, squirrel, raccoon, woodchuck, and wild turkey — was essential on the frontier. In New England, salt fish, oysters, and clams were the staples. Pigs were kept almost everywhere. Those who could afford them kept chickens and cows and enjoyed eggs, milk, butter, and cheese as well as meat from their animals.

Fresh meat was generally roasted. Some households had iron turning spits to cook large pieces. Others made do with a contraption of heavy cords, twisted hard, that was hung from the mantelpiece. Once the cord was twisted it would wind up and down easily so that all sides of the meat suspended from it in front of the fire would cook evenly. A dripping pan was placed on the hearth underneath, and a Yorkshire pudding or spoon bread might be cooked in it.

The fall of the year was the busiest season for both men and women as the men brought in their harvest and the women put up the produce for the winter. It was in the fall that cows and pigs were slaughtered. This would be done early in the frosty morning so that the meat would be hard and cold for processing. The methods of preserving food were taught to girls by their mothers or mistresses. Printed cookbooks were rare. Where recipes were written down they are more apt to appear in handwritten books. These give us a fascinating glimpse at the activities inside an eighteenth-century kitchen. Here are the directions for preserving beef and beef tongues. Note the large quantities required:

> For ½ barrel take say 2½ doz. tongues, say 100 lbs. Beef 3 or 4 lbs. Common Brown Sugar. Cover the bottom of the barrel with fine salt. Then rub the pieces with Saltpetre. Put them in thight, forming one layer. Over this throw a good quantity of fine salt and then about the same quantity of sugar. Upon this place the second layer and cover it as before rubbing each piece with a little Saltpetre, before placing in and so on. ¼ lb. of Saltpetre is enough for a half barrel. Place a heavy stone upon the top of the whole which serves to keep the beef tight and cool and under the brine. Wait a few

days before putting in the brine and see what brine is made and then make sufficient to cover the whole. For the brine take a pint of salt to a common bucket of water.

When such salt meat was cooked later on it had to be soaked in warm water for a long while before it would be edible. Then it was commonly boiled in a kettle placed at the side of the fire where the temperature was lower. If cooked at high heat the meat was too tough to chew. Salt meat was frequently served with boiled vegetables.

The winter vegetables were not canned. Such a method was too time-consuming. Root vegetables, such as potatoes, turnips, and carrots, were buried under earth or sand in the cellar. Corn, beans, pumpkins, and squash were preserved by drying. Even fruit, such as peaches, plums, and apples were usually dried rather than put up in sugar or molasses syrup. On the other hand, the monotony of winter meals and the strong, not altogether pleasant smell and flavor of salt meat, made Americans extremely fond of pickles and relishes. Onions, cucumbers, asparagus, mushrooms, walnuts, and even nasturtium buds were pickled. They were put up in large stone crocks sealed with congealed fat and covered with an animal bladder or a bit of leather.

Winter and summer, corn in some form appeared on the table of almost every American family at every meal. Corn grew in all parts of the country. It was much easier to raise and process than such alternatives as wheat, barley, rice, or rye. There were hundreds of ways to prepare it. It might be steamed, roasted, broiled, or popped. Most of it, however, was ground into meal at a local water mill or by hand with mortar and pestle devices. Ground meal might be mixed with water and boiled into a mush for "hasty pudding." Mixed with butter, sugar, eggs, mace, and nutmeg, with a bit of wine or rum stirred in made an elegant dessert pudding. Or the mush could be fried on a griddle to make "Johnny cake" or "corn pone." Men going off to the field or children going to school would put a few of these hot cakes in their pockets or hats to keep themselves warm. Later in the day they could be eaten for lunch. The famous Boston brown bread was also made of corn meal.

White wheat bread and cakes were an upper class luxury. Wheat was difficult to grow and yeast had to be nurtured with as much attention as the fire to keep it active. Pies, however, were common and were eaten at every meal. They might be filled with meat, vegetables, fruit, or any combination, and the crusts were of cornmeal.

The beverage that accompanied colonial meals was usually alcoholic. Rum cut with water — "grog" — was consumed in large quantities by men, women, and children. Whiskey, hard cider, ale, beer, wines, and cordials were also produced in colonial households. The thirst produced by eating so much salt meat and fish, the need for calories to work hard and keep warm during the winter, as well as a belief in the medicinal qualities of alcohol, convinced colonial Americans that rum was a necessity of life.

The hard-working women of colonial America found cooking their most difficult and time-consuming chore. They cut corners wherever they could, for it was all they could do to get something on the table without wasting time on refinements. They were generally considered to be terrible cooks. Although Americans of the eighteenth century had plenty of food available, they suffered from dietary deficiencies and diseases because of its poor preparation. It is no accident that the "typical" American, Uncle Sam, is pictured as lean, bony, and hungry-looking. The overweight American is a recent development. Colonial Americans bolted down their food and did not expect to enjoy it. It was reported in 1758 that in America "House pie, in the country places, is made of apples neither peeled nor freed from their cores, and its crust is not broken if a wagon wheel goes over it."

Until late in the eighteenth century dishes were scarce. A woman might own a few treasured pewter pieces, but wooden trenchers — made by the men and boys when they could spare the time — were much more common. Some family meals were served in a single bowl from which everyone helped himself with the assistance of knives, fingers, and chunks of bread. Some families had no benches for their dining table and stood during their meals. Wealthy families, of course, had many kitchen servants, china dishes, silver table service, and fine dining room furniture. These individuals dined in the manner of upper-class Europeans, and even their servants, slaves, and children who ate in the kitchen enjoyed better meals than most Americans.

After feeding the family, making clothing was the colonial woman's most urgent chore. Although, like cooking, it was a necessity, colonial women appear to have taken much pleasure in this activity. The product was tangible while meals disappeared as soon as they were put on the table. Furthermore, cooking involved very dirty work, sweating over a blazing fire and poking through the ashes with no company except children and servants. Many of the processes involved in producing clothing could be accomplished while seated comfortably out of doors or in the parlor enjoying the company of friends and neighbors. By contrast, then, making clothing was a pleasure for women. It was the closest thing they had to a leisure activity. They put much thought and effort into making their handwork original and beautiful as well as functional.

The most popular clothing material for lower-class people was leather or fur, since it required no weaving. Advertisements for runaway servants and slaves show about a third of them wearing leather clothing. Even well-to-do people often owned a few garments made of leather. Leather was a by-product wherever there was

hunting. The tanning techniques, which were learned
from the Indians, were relatively simple.

Flax, from which linen is made, grew wild in America.
Yet it was far harder to produce linen shirts or petticoats
than to make them of leather. It took at least sixteen
months from the planting of flax seed to the production of
the finished cloth. Young flax plants are very tender.
The women and children who weeded had to be
extremely careful, for the least bruise would kill the
plants. Mature plants were picked and dried. Then the
seeds were teased out with coarse combs, and the gluey
substance in the fibers was removed by repeated washings. Finally the flax fibers were separated from the
waste by picking and combing. Only then could spinning begin.

The loose brown filaments of flax were twisted
together to form thread. This was done at spinning
wheels, frequently homemade, which used weights to
twist the filaments under tension. The aim was to
produce as fine a thread as possible. The fingers of a
skilled spinner might produce more than forty miles of
thread from a pound of fiber. The threads were wound
into skeins called "knots." At this point the thread was
light brown in color. Cloth woven from it would be
quite serviceable. Most women, however, having done so
much already, put in the additional time needed to make
the serviceable cloth beautiful as well. They began by
bleaching the knots. The techniques involved, like those

of cooking, were taught to girls by older women. Thirty or forty washings in hot water were necessary with the addition of such other ingredients as potash, lime, or buttermilk. When the knots were white enough they were dried and then dyed.

Dyeing was a skill highly valued by colonial women. They passed on their coloring recipes as family treasures. During the winter, when there was less work to do, women worked out new formulas that produced different shades with good resistance to fading. They discovered, for instance, that onion skins boiled in a brass kettle would produce lemon yellow thread while onion skins boiled in an iron kettle produced a gold yellow. For a greenish yellow shade, St. John's wort and alum were boiled together. Skeins of dyed thread were kept in bags tied with sample rags showing the color inside and the recipe was frequently attached. Such thread was then available for elaborate embroidery projects as well as for winding on the loom.

Wool cloth was slightly easier to produce than linen but still difficult. After the sheep were sheared the fleece was picked through and brambles and other dirt removed. Then the wool was washed and dried and pork fat was rubbed into it. Next the wool was combed with a wool-card, which pulled the fibres into parallel rows that could be lifted out, spun into thread, and dyed as the flax was. A cloth made of a combination of linen and wool, called linsey-woolsey, was very popular in colonial America.

While some women by the late eighteenth century might turn their skeins of thread over to a professional weaver, many still made their own cloth at home. If the household was very large a special weaving house might be built to accommodate the loom. The warp of the fabric was laid on the loom by hand, each thread placed precisely and held at a constant tension. The weaving itself consisted of pressing a foot treadle to separate the warp threads, throwing a threaded shuttle between them, and finally swinging down a batten to push the thread tight. Since this work was done in spare moments between other chores, it might easily take a year for a wife to make her husband a cloth suit. Such a garment was highly valued by its owner. It would be worn only on special occasions, mended when it became worn, remade for a son, and finally turned into patchwork.

Not all clothing was woven. Stockings, mittens, and caps were knitted. Knitting was a constant feminine occupation. Little girls began to make stockings and mittens as soon as they could hold the needles, and elderly grandmothers, who were too feeble and blind to do any other work, still kept their hands occupied with their needles. Wealthy women as well as poor automatically reached for their knitting whenever they sat down.

Quilting, appliqué, patchwork, crewel work, and silk

embroidery were skills commonly cultivated by colonial women. They could be used to decorate useful articles such as petticoats, bed hangings, and upholstery. They might also be used to create pictures for the wall. Upper-class women had formal education in needlework and produced fine work in good perspective with stitches much smaller and more lustrous than could be produced with paint and brush. Most girls and women of the upper classes had some such project at hand to be picked up during their leisure time or on social occasions. Little girls took their sewing baskets along when they went off with their brothers on a children's picnic. Mercy Otis Warren, the playwright and historian, missed her needle-work as much as her writing when she injured a finger and could not use her hand.

If producing the family's clothing might be a pleasure, cleaning was never anything but drudgery. Fortunately for the colonial woman, who already had great demands on her time, the standards of the eighteenth century were not high. It was thought appropriate that human beings, like other animals, should smell. People washed their hands and faces but bathed only rarely. Too much bathing was considered unhealthy — which it probably was when done in cold water in an unheated house during a New England winter. A Philadelphia lady who tried a newly designed shower bath in 1771 found being "wet all over at once" such an unpleasant experience that she did not repeat the experiment for twenty-eight years.

Clothing was rarely laundered except among the very wealthy. Most people did not own many garments, and wash day came only once or twice a year.

Neither of the essentials for cleaning — water or soap — was easily available to the colonial homemaker. Towns had public pumps or water carts from which water could be purchased. Fortunate families had a well, spring, or clean brook near their home. Others, however, might have to carry their buckets a mile or more to bring water into the house. Furthermore, water pollution was not unknown even in colonial days. A visitor to a settlement in Kentucky reported in 1780: "The Spring at this place is below the Fort and fed by ponds above the Fort so that the whole dirt and filth of the Fort, putrified flesh, dead dogs, horse, cow, hog excrements and human odour all wash into the spring which with the Ashes and sweepings of filthy Cabbins, the dirtiness of the people, steeping skins to dress and washing every sort of dirty rags and cloths in the spring perfectly poisons the water and makes the most filthy nauseous potation of the water imaginable . . ."

Soap was made of lye and animal fat. The first ingredient was obtained by collecting ashes from hard wood burned in the fireplace in raised tubs with small holes in the bottom. The ashes were covered with water and lye leaked through the holes into tubs placed underneath. In making soap it was important to have the lye the right strength. As with other feminine skills, judging the strength of the lye was a trick passed on from mother to daughter. One old recipe stated, "If your Lye will bear up an Egg or a Potato so you can see a piece of the Surface as big as a Ninepence it is just strong enough."

While the ashes were being collected, the housewife also saved animal grease. After several months, when enough had been accumulated, it was put in kettles over a hot fire, preferably out of doors, and the tubs of lye were poured in. This was a lethal potion, which could easily serve as a weapon when a soapmaker was surprised by an Indian. The mixture jellied into what was called soft soap and was then stored in tubs. It was used for cleaning clothing, kettles, and people's hands and faces. The rosy cheeks we see on portraits of colonial Americans were due more often to the action of lye soap than to a condition of blooming health.

The interior of the home of a poor family was dirtier than that of a prosperous family, but neither would pass inspection by a modern visitor. The poorest families in the backwoods lived in log cabins. The walls were covered with bits of bark and mud. The floor was bare earth and was always either dusty or damp. The furniture consisted of a rough plank table — one or two rough slabs of wood laid on a trestle — a few stools or benches, and a great many beds. When a family was large and the cabin small, it was often necessary for several people to sleep in one bed. Mattresses were made of straw. Featherbeds or quilts stuffed with straw or cotton provided warmth. The most urgent cleaning problem was apt to be dealing with vermin — fleas, lice, and bedbugs. The most effective solution was to burn the bedding.

Middle-class people, especially those in the towns, lived a great deal better. By the end of the colonial period wealthy families had wallpaper, mirrors, carpets, fine furniture, sheets and pillow cases for their beds, and elaborate bed draperies to keep out the night air, which was thought to be unwholesome. Even in these homes, however, it was not possible to spare the labor to keep them as we see them today when they are open to visitors as restorations.

Fortunately for the peace of mind of the colonial Americans, they had very indistinct ideas about the connection between dirt and disease. They were, however, well acquainted with the symptoms of a great many deadly maladies. The treatment of these, as well as of wounds and accidental injuries of all sorts, was largely the responsibility of women.

America was a sickly place throughout the colonial period. The diseases of three continents — Europe, Africa, and America — met in the British colonies. Unsanitary living conditions and poor diet left the population susceptible to every wandering germ. Among the diseases that raged in North America during the Revolutionary era were malaria, dysentery, typhoid fever, yellow fever, tuberculosis, cholera, diphtheria, typhus, measles, whooping cough, scarlet fever, influenza, smallpox, and countless unidentified "fluxes" and "fevers."

University-trained physicians were in short supply in America. That, however, was probably fortunate. Medical education was based on the writings of the ancient Greeks. The treatments prescribed were frequently more deadly than the disease. Bloodletting (with an unsterile instrument), blistering, and violent purges and emetics were recommended for everything from headaches to yellow fever.

In the eighteenth century, however, there was an alternative to the medicine taught by European universities — the medicine practiced by "old wives" and passed on from mother to daughter. In view of the painful and frequently fatal treatments prescribed by physicians, it is no wonder that most Americans preferred to submit themselves to the herbal remedies of women. If they did not prolong life, they might at least make death less painful.

Women took their medical responsibilities seriously. They learned their skills by experience — assisting their mothers tend the sick and injured before they took over households of their own — and by studying manuscript recipe books. When colonial women spoke of recipes — or "receipts" — they meant medical prescriptions and directions for making fabric dyes more often than they meant instructions for preparing food. Martha Washington's handwritten recipe book contains the following prescription for "Capon Ale," which is recommended as a treatment for tuberculosis:

> Take an old Capon with yellow Leggs pull him and crush ye bones, but keep ye skin whole and then take an ounce of carraway seeds, and an ounce of anny seeds and two ounces of harts horne and one handful of rosemary tops, a piece or 2 of mace and a Leamon pill. Sow all these into ye bellie of your Capon & chop him into hot mash or hot water and put him into two gallons of strong ale when it is working, after let it stand for two or three dayes & put a lump of sugar into every bottle wh will make it drink brisker.

Swallowing a pint of this alcoholic chicken soup might not cure a consumptive, but it would certainly leave him feeling better than he would after being leached of a pint of blood.

Colonial women also studied medical texts. A surprisingly large number of colonial women could read — far more could read than could write — and the most popular reading material after the Bible and religious tracts was medical literature. Some of these books had been written by women, particularly texts on obstetrics and gynecology.

Until well into the eighteenth century, delivering

babies was the exclusive province of women. Male
midwives, known as "accouchers," appeared after the
middle of the eighteenth century, but most Americans
distrusted them and preferred to continue with the
women they knew. Many women had extremely large
families. Mothers of fourteen, fifteen, and even twenty
children were not unheard of. Many women also died in
childbirth, however, and the infant mortality rate was
appalling.

The high death rate among young children in colonial
America was due partly to uncontrolled epidemics of
such diseases as measles and diphtheria. But much of it
was due to the child-care practices of colonial mothers.
Indeed, it is in their relationship with their children,
which seems to us unfeeling and frequently cruel, that
colonial women appear most alien to our time.

Adults of the eighteenth century thought of children as
animals or servants, not as human beings. Furthermore,
they did not believe children would develop into human
beings unless they were forced to it. It was their nature
to be sinful and animalistic. Consequently permitting a
child to follow its natural inclinations in any way was
considered the sign of a bad parent. Rather than trying to
encourage independence and personal development in
their offspring, colonial parents worked to break the
child's spirit. For instance, it was noted that infants
preferred crawling on all fours to walking upright. In
order to discourage such "animal" behavior, a crawling

infant was put in a "go cart," a sort of cage that came up
to its armpits and forced it to stand. An alternative was to
tie the child with "leading strings" fastened to the
shoulders that would hold it upright.

As a popular book on child rearing explained, "Parents
should carefully subdue the wills of their children and
accustom them to obedience and submission." In order to
accomplish this children were whipped. Mothers used
sticks hard enough to cause bruises and swelling on their
children even before they were old enough to talk. A
young mother wrote to a friend in 1755:

> I have begun to govern Sally. She has been
> whipped once on *Old Adams'* account, and she
> knows the difference between a smile and a frown
> as well as I do. When she has done anything that
> she suspects is wrong [she] will look with concern
> to see what Momma says . . . although she is not
> quite ten months old, yet when she knows so much
> I think 'tis time she should be taught.

Children might also be punished by being tied to their
beds, threatened with ghosts and monsters, or be shut up
for hours in dark closets or chests.

Scarcely better than punishment was the treatment to
which children were subjected for their health. It was
considered good practice to "toughen" young children by
giving them frequent cold baths even in the coldest

weather, to starve them in order to discourage what was thought an inclination in youngsters to overeat, and even to put them into iron collars or strap them to boards to encourage them to grow up straight.

Mothers who thus abused their children both physically and psychologically believed that they were acting for the children's good. They felt it was necessary to train their children to be obedient, respectful, well-mannered, and hard workers. Colonial mothers had no antipathy to child labor; on the contrary, they encouraged it. Play was viewed with suspicion. When children were too young to work in the field or help in the kitchen, mothers were advised to keep them indoors studying a book or learning to knit or embroider rather than allowing them to go outside and cultivate their animal instincts toward idleness.

By the time they were seven or eight, children of all social classes were frequently sent to live with a relative or bound out as apprentices. It was felt the natural mother might be reluctant to discipline her child with the desirable strictness. A colonial woman, then, often had both her own younger children and children of others in her home to train and supervise at their work. By working for an adult, children of both sexes learned those skills necessary to run a household and earn a living. By the time children were grown they had generally done enough work to pay for their keep and education and produce a profit for their parents as well.

It seems a grim enough childhood to us today. Those who experienced it, however, thought it the only proper upbringing. Little girls grew up and married and proceeded to train their own children just as they had been trained.

2

WOMEN'S WORK: MAKING MONEY

IN POOR FAMILIES in colonial America, homemaking might be a full-time job for both men and women. On a subsistence farm with no cash income, the family produced everything it consumed and consumed everything it produced. All work was directly related to meeting the needs of the family. But few Americans remained on the subsistence level. In order to enjoy a higher standard of living, members of a family would specialize in a profit-making occupation. By producing an excess of some article they could barter or buy other household essentials from other families. Thus a man whose hunting skill produced more meat and skins than his family needed could sell the excess. A woman whose handling of cows and chickens was superior would soon be earning "butter and egg money." Colonial Americans believed in the virtues of thrift, frugality, and hard work. Consequently, when they earned a bit of money they did not spend all of it to improve their standard of living. Instead, a good part of such income would be reinvested. A woman might use her butter and egg money, for instance, to buy another cow. But there were other choices. Since both men and women began their adult life with a variety of skills, accumulated savings could be used for other purposes. The superior dairywoman, for instance, might use her funds to buy a large loom and become a professional weaver, taking in spun yarn produced by her neighbors and turning it into cloth for a fee. In this way a household industry was born.

By the time of the American Revolution, the economy of the colonies had become fairly complex. Most people made their living from the land, but farming certainly was not the only occupation available. In addition to shipwrights, fishermen, and practitioners of a variety of crafts, there were shopkeepers, barbers, tavern-keepers, and people in other service occupations. Just as on a farm, however, these were household businesses. Husband, wife, children, servants, and apprentices worked as a team. In a preindustrial age few occupations could be carried out by any single individual working alone. The many stages required in cloth production, for example, required the labor of a number of people if a weaver's operation was to produce cloth in large enough quantities for sale. Although the husband was recognized as the legal head of any household business, women were often as skilled in the operation as the men. It was not uncommon for a daughter of the family to marry an apprentice and carry on the business to which both had been trained. It was quite common for a widow to carry on the business after her husband's death. Because of this arrangement, there was no occupation in colonial America from which women were excluded. Every kind of work done by men was done, at least occasionally, by women.

Running a farm or plantation was the most common business enterprise for women, as it was for men. Women's names are recorded as landowners from the earliest days of settlement. Captain John Smith described the achievements of an early Virginia planter who returned to London in 1629: "Mistress *Pearce*, an honest industrious woman, hath beene there [in Virginia] neere twentie yeares, and now returned, saith, shee hath a garden at *James* towne containing three or four acres, where in one year shee hath gathered neere an hundred bushels of excellent figges, and that of her own provision she can keepe a better house in *Virginia*, than here in *London* . . . yet [she] went thither with little or nothing." Half a century later another Englishman staying at the home of "a very acute, ingenious lady," described his hostess and other women planters in Virginia who grew tobacco, drained swampland, raised cattle, and bought and sold slaves. Seventeenth-century court records reveal many women registering deeds for farmland, indenturing servants, suing for debts due them or being sued by others. In the eighteenth century, newspaper advertisements allow us to study the activities of women involved in large-scale agriculture. They advertised land, horses, and slaves for sale, offered rewards for runaway slaves, and demanded payment from those who owed them money. For instance, Sarah Blakeley's name appeared frequently in the advertisements run by the *South Carolina Gazette*. At various times she had houses for rent, slaves for hire, and was willing to sell such things as land, Indian corn, and slaves. When she left the province in 1741 and liquidated her holdings she advertised several houses and lots, farmland and slaves, several beds, a set of mahogany chairs, a spinet, and some books. At the same time she advertised for a business agent to represent her at Cape Fear.

Most commonly the women found running plantations or large farms were widows. They appear to have managed the business as well and sometimes better than the men. Mary Willing Byrd, widow of William Byrd III of Virginia, is an outstanding example. Although Byrd had inherited a large estate he was given to gambling and had no head for business. He left his affairs in great confusion. His widow was left to salvage what property she could for herself and the eight children of the marriage. A French visitor described her remarkable success: "She has preserved his beautiful house, situated on James-River, a large personal property, a considerable number of slaves, and some plantations which she has rendered valuable. She is about two-and-forty, with an agreeable countenance and great sense. . . . Her care and activity have in some measure repaired the effects of her husband's dissipation and her house is still the most celebrated, and the most agreeable of the neighborhood."

Other women, however, were left in charge when husbands or fathers were absent from home for long periods. Eliza Lucas Pinckney, for example, is deservedly the best-known colonial woman planter. She was responsible for beginning the production of indigo in South Carolina. Indigo is the basis of a blue dye, which was much in demand among British cloth manufacturers. It was one of the most important export crops of the colony before the Revolution. Eliza Lucas began to run her father's plantations at the age of seventeen. Her father was a British army officer who was ordered to the West Indies and her mother was too ill to take over the management of the property. Eliza, as she said, "loved the vegetable world extremely." When the business affairs of three plantations allowed her time, she conducted agricultural experiments. She was only twenty-one when her indigo experiment, proving that the plant could be grown in South Carolina, was successful. She married

Colonel Charles Pinckney the same year. During their marriage she continued her experiments. She was particularly interested in cultivating silk worms. After her husband's death in 1758 she again resumed full control of her property and his as well.

Not every widow was fortunate enough to inherit land. In order to support themselves unattached women often sought work in a farm family. White women servants did not usually work in the fields, although they might in an emergency. But they were willing to do all kinds of "women's work" for pay. Thus advertisements such as the following frequently ran in colonial newspapers: "A single woman, with a child, would be glad of a place on a plantation, to take charge of a dairy, raise poultry etc." Another advertised "A Dairy Woman who can make negro clothes wants work." Potential employers advertised for women who could spin, sew, manage a kitchen, and do other tasks usually the responsibility of the mistress of the house. A man who was wealthy enough could hire someone to do the "women's work" in his home if his wife became ill or if he was a widower who preferred not to remarry. Thomas Hanson Marshall of Maryland, for example, advertised for "a Woman that is qualified for managing Household Affairs and bringing up Girls, in a Genteel Way." Similarly, wealthy widows advertised for male servants to do the work that had formerly been a husband's responsibility.

Farming was most profitable in the South and in the

middle colonies. In New England the largest fortunes were usually made in trade or some sort of manufacturing. As in planting, the women who ran businesses on their own were usually widows. In some areas, however, the men's activities might require them to be absent from home so often and for such long periods that most business enterprises were run by the wives. This was the case, for instance, on the island of Nantucket. The chief occupation of Nantucket men was fishing or whaling. They might spend many months or even years at a time at sea. A few wives accompanied the men on these voyages, doing "women's work" at sea or acting as navigators. But most remained at home and ran businesses of their own. Hector St. John de Crèvecoeur, a Frenchman settled in America, was greatly impressed by the business capacity of Nantucket wives. "As the sea excursions are often very long, their wives in their absence are necessarily obliged to transact business, to settle accounts, and, in short, to rule and provide for their families," he wrote. "These circumstances, being often repeated, give women the abilities as well as a taste for the kind of superintendency to which, by their prudence and good management, they seem to be in general very equal. This employment ripens their judgment, and justly entitles them to a rank superior to other wives." Married women needed their husband's consent to all legal transactions, but this was no problem for Nantucket wives. "The men at their return, weary with the fatigues of the sea, . . . cheerfully give their consent to every transaction that has happened during their absence, and all is joy and peace. 'Wife, thee hast done well,' is the general approbation they receive, for their application and industry." When a wife worked independently of her husband, as those of Nantucket did, her contribution to the family prosperity was even more apparent than when she merely assisted her husband in a business he directed. Thus Crèvecoeur noted that "The richest person now in the island owes all his present prosperity and success to the ingenuity of his wife: . . . for while he was performing his first cruises, she traded with pins and needles, and kept a school. Afterward she purchased more considerable articles, which she sold with so much judgment, that she laid the foundation of a system of business, that she has ever since prosecuted with equal dexterity and success."

Women who succeeded to ownership of a business placed advertisements in their own names in colonial newspapers. These advertisements illustrate the wide variety of business activities open to women in the Revolutionary era. They participated more fully in the economic life of their day than women have since, even in our own century.

Widow Manikin, a Philadelphia apothecary, announced her shop could supply "things as are principally used in the Modern Practice of Physick, being a great variety of Materia Medica, both simple and compound."

In Virginia, Sarah Watson sold "an excellent eye water" that she confidently promised would cure "specks, cataracts, and strengthen weak eyes." At her shop one might also purchase perfumed soap balls, lip salves, and an almond paste for the hands.

Women barbers were quite common. Men who traveled through the colonies frequently noted that they were "shaved by the barber's wife." In addition to shaving men and powdering their hair, barbers practiced minor surgery such as pulling teeth or opening the veins of patients for whom bleeding was prescribed. They might also make simple wigs. However, to prepare elaborate headdresses for wealthy women who wished to copy European fashions, professional hairdressers were employed. These towering headpieces were not approved by most women of the Revolutionary era. They were expensive luxuries, and so not suitable for frugal and patriotic women, and they were also uncomfortable and inconvenient. It took hours to build up a stiff and powdered hairdo. Women therefore let one dressing do for a month or more. The powder quickly attracted vermin, to deal with which the lady purchased a "wig pick." It also attracted mice when the lady slept at night. To deal with this threat a special wire cage was worn over the hairdo at night.

Independent women blacksmiths advertised occasionally. In 1754 the newly widowed Mary Salmon of Boston announced that she would "carry on the business of horse-shoeing, as theretofore, where all gentlemen may have their Horses shod in the best Manner, as also all sorts of Blacksmith's Work done with Fidelity and Dispatch." Similarly Jane Burgess, a Maryland widow, announced in 1773, "I still carry on the Blacksmith Business, and shall be obliged to my Friends for the continuance of their Favours." Women learned to stand the heat and built up a good bit of muscle power in their usual kitchen activities. Blacksmithing, however, is a skilled job that requires training. These widows clearly had participated in the work while their husbands were still alive.

Other widows advertised their foundry work. A few owned forges. There were a number of women gun-smiths. Mary Jackson of Boston was a tinker and advertised that she could make "Tea-Kettles and coffee pots, copper Drinking Pots, Brass and copper Sauce-Pans, stew-pans, Baking-pans, Kettle-pots and Fish Kettles." Elizabeth Russell of South Carolina was a shipwright. Mary Butler of Maryland would supply her customers with blocks for ships and would make pumps for ships. Temperance Grant of Rhode Island carried on the family shipping business for twenty-two years after she was widowed in 1744. At least one woman took over her husband's whaler. Her account book records a month in which her share was fifty-two barrels of whale oil: "Feb. ye 4, Indian Harry, with his boat, struck a stunt whale and could not kill it, — called my boat to help him.

I had but a third, which was 4 barrels. Feb. 22, my two boats, and my son's, and Floyd's boats, killed a yearling whale of which I had half, — made 36, my share 18 barrels. Feb. 24, my company killed a small yearling, made 30 barrels."

There were also a good number of women sextons who were paid to maintain the churchyard, ring the bell for services, and dig graves. Several jails were maintained by women.

Because of the social and political importance of the press, women in the printing business have attracted more attention than those in any other occupation. The first press to be brought to America was owned by a woman. She and her husband brought it over from England, but he died on the way. At the time of the Revolution about a dozen women were owners of printing establishments. Other women, wives and daughters of owners, set type, helped in the shop, or ran the bookshops or stationery stores that printers usually maintained as a sideline. Deborah Read Franklin ran the print shop of her husband, Benjamin Franklin, when he was out of the country. There were a number of women printers in the Franklin family. His sister-in-law, Anne Smith Franklin, had been named state printer of Rhode Island in 1736 and became publisher of the *Newport Mercury* in 1762. Margaret H. Bache, the wife of Franklin's grandson Benjamin Franklin Bache, published

The Aurora in Philadelphia after her husband's death in
1798.

The Goddards were another prominent printing family. Sarah Updike Goddard of Providence, Rhode Island,
lent her son William enough money to start the *Providence Gazette* in 1765 and then became his partner. A few
years later William Goddard and his sister Mary Katherine Goddard went to Baltimore. They bought out the
printing business that Nicholas Hasselbaugh had be-
queathed to his widow and that she had been carrying on
alone. The two Goddards began to publish the *Maryland
Journal* and Baltimore *Advertiser* in 1773. Since her
brother had other interests, Mary Katherine Goddard did
most of the work. She was chosen by Congress to print
the official copy of the Declaration of Independence in
1776. Later she became postmistress of Baltimore and
operated a bookstore and a paper mill in addition to her
publishing activities. She was one of the few unmarried
colonial women to achieve economic independence.

Women who participated in the family businesses just
described had to be trained to tasks unrelated to the
"women's" activities that every little girl learned from
her mother. Other family businesses, however, developed as extensions of "women's work." Selling goods of
various sorts, for instance, seemed to women a very
natural occupation, and women demonstrated a great
confidence in their ability when they opened up shops.

The merchants' guilds both in England and on the continent of Europe had admitted women. Women apparently anticipated no difficulty in keeping books and calculating profits. Occasionally, women built wharves, which would attract ships to a shop or other related business.

Sometimes they sold products they made themselves. Such was the case with a woman of Wilmington, North Carolina, who was described by a visitor in 1775: "The Mrs. of this place is a pattern of industry, . . . She has (it seems) a garden, from which she supplies the town with what vegetables they use, also with mellons and other fruits. She even descends to make minced pies, tarts, and cheesecakes and little biskets, which she sends down to town once or twice a day, besides her eggs, poultry, and butter, and she is the only one who continues to have Milk." This woman had found an ingenious way to avoid problems with creditors: "All her little commodities are contrived so as not to exceed one penny a piece, and her customers know she will not run tick, which were they to run by the length of sixpence must be the case, as that is a sum not in everybody's power, and she must be paid by some other articles, whereas the two coppers, (that is, half pence) are ready money." Other women featured luxury items imported from abroad. Madame Le Mercier, whose shop was on Back Street in Boston, advertised during the Revolution that she stocked "every sort of Beauties, just received from France." When the war was over, and importing from England could resume, Margaret Phillips of Boston announced her "large and beautiful assortment of Picked Goods," from London. Women importers appeared in all the major port towns.

The operation of a tavern involved little more than homemaking on a larger scale. Most taverns were run by husband and wife, but perhaps as many as a third were run by women alone. A widow who inherited her home and perhaps some house slaves, but little land, or who felt unable to make a living by farming, would find taking in lodgers and entertaining travelers an obvious means of support. With a few improvements — putting in a billiard table, setting up a bar, and stocking the cellar with plenty of rum, wine, and beer — a woman was ready to apply for a license and hang out a sign. Women who ran taverns near a body of water might assure the popularity of their establishments if they could arrange to be appointed manager of a public ferry.

Colonial taverns served a number of functions in the community. In addition to providing lodging for strangers, they were meeting places for local businessmen and centers of social life. Men held their political meetings in taverns. Cock fights and lottery drawings were held there. The stagecoaches that brought travelers also brought news from the outside world and copies of newspapers from other towns in America. The tavern was therefore the center of information in a community. The tavernkeeper frequently became a political power in

the town. A Georgia lawyer remembered Nancy Rumsey, who had started her career by keeping a "traveling
restaurant." On the day the court met she brought her
oxcart to the town square. The back of the cart would be
pulled down to reveal a large barrel of hard cider. Then
she set up a table with cups, a box of gingerbread, and a
bag of chestnuts. All the lawyers in the county were
soon regular customers. When she had earned enough
money she bought a house and set up a tavern. Every
man running for public office wanted her support because
her political contacts had become more extensive than
those of any other person in the county. For half a
century, it was said, Nancy Rumsey was the boss of
Elbert County, Georgia.

The quality of colonial taverns varied as greatly as did
the quality of colonial homes. A gentleman traveling in
upper New York State was delighted by the tavern in
Little Falls. He praised the breakfast table set with
"table-cloth, tea tray, tea-pots, milk-pot, bowls, cups,
sugartongs, casters, plates, knives, forks, tea, sugar,
cream, bread, butter, steak, eggs, cheese, potatoes, beets,
salt, vinegar, pepper and all for twenty five cents." At
the other extreme was "Mrs. Teaze's Tavern," which
was visited by the Marquis de Chastellux. He reported
that "a solitary tin vessel was the only bowl for the
family, the servants and ourselves." Mary Davis of
Williamsburg kept her tavern in "Dr. Carter's large
brick house," which was obviously comfortable and

convenient: "She has 12 or 14 very good lodging rooms, with fireplaces to most of them, which will hold two or three beds each . . . The rooms above are convenient for Gentlemen, those below for Ladies; the house consisting of two parts, and divided lengthwise by a brick partition." On the other hand, the tavern on the road between Greenville and Tarboro, North Carolina, consisted of two rooms. The sitting room had a dirt floor and one bed. The bedroom had a board floor and contained four beds. The proprietor was an elderly woman, eighty-four years old. She did all the work herself, including caring for the guests' horses.

Perhaps typical of country tavernkeepers was Elizabeth Flanagan of Four Corners, New York. She was immortalized in James Fenimore Cooper's novel *The Spy*. Although her inn was made the scene of an incident in a work of fiction, she herself was a real character. "Her faults," Cooper wrote, "were a trifling love of liquor, excessive filthiness, and a total disregard of all the decencies of language; her virtues, an unbounded love for her adopted country, perfect honesty when dealing on certain known principles with the soldiery, and great good-nature. Added to these, Betty had the merit of being the inventor of that beverage which is so well known at the present hour . . . which is distinguished by the name of 'cock-tail.' Elizabeth Flanagan was peculiarly well qualified, by education and circumstance to perfect this improvement in liquors, having been literally brought up on its principal ingredient." Mrs. Flanagan's cocktail was a combination of rum, rye, and fruit juice. On one occasion during the Revolution she was said to have served it to a French officer decorated with a feather pulled from the tail of a Tory neighbor's rooster. The Frenchman, delighted with the concoction, gave the toast, "Vive le Coq's Tail!"

The women who ran taverns applied the ability to manage a large household to the work of caring for strangers. A similar extension of "women's work" is apparent in the occupations of women who advertised as butchers, bakers, brewers, confectioners, dressmakers, laundresses, and tanners. The practice of medicine fell into the same category. Caring for the sick was considered natural "women's work" as was delivery of babies.

Before the Revolution and the establishment of regular medical schools in America, there were no restrictions on women who wished to practice "physick" and "chirurgery." As late as 1796 it was reported that no male physician had ever practiced in Cape May County, New Jersey. "Medicine," it was said, "has been administered by women, except in extraordinary cases." Because it was so common for housewives to care for the sick and injured in their own families, few professional doctors of either sex could expect to make a living by practicing medicine. It was usually a side line. Upper-class women used their healing talents to earn a little extra income; poorer women would practice medicine to supplement their earnings from other sources. Thus William Byrd, when describing the principal inhabitants of the town of Fredericksburg, wrote, "I must not forget Mrs. Levistone, who Acts here in the double Capacity of a Doctress and Coffee Woman." It was considered quite proper for doctors to advertise their cures in the newspapers. In October, 1766, the *Virginia Gazette* printed testimonials from patients of Constant Woodson who, it was said, had cured them of cancer. About the same time, Mary Adams of South Carolina was advertising her cures for "the blind and all disorders in the eyes." A certain Mrs. Kayser of Maryland declared that her remedy for ague would effect "a cure in three days" and her "charge for the cure is only *Five Shillings*." Mrs. Hughes of Virginia, whose specialty was "Ringworms, Scald Heads, Sore Eyes, the Piles, Worms in Children, and several other Disorders," promised her patients *"No Cure, No Pay."*

Although practicing medicine was rarely a full-time occupation, midwifery was. Eighteenth-century America had a fast-growing population. Obituaries of midwives often identify them as having delivered thousands of children in the course of their careers. In 1771 a Williamsburg, Virginia, paper recorded the passing of "Mrs. Catherine Blaikley, of this City, in the seventy-sixth year of her Age; an eminent Midwife, and who, in the course of her Practice, brought upwards of three Thousand Children into the World." Her record was surpassed by a South Carolina practitioner: "Tuesday last died, greatly lamented, aged 73 years, Mrs. Elizabeth Hunt, a native of this province, and practising midwife. — It is said to appear, by an account regularly kept by her, that she had been present at the birth of near 4000 children."

Midwifery was traditionally a woman's profession. Although most midwives had no formal training, a surprising number of those who advertised in the last half of the eighteenth century had attended European medical schools. Thus a Mrs. Grant, who established a practice in Charleston, South Carolina, announced that she had studied at Edinburgh and could produce letters from "the Gentlemen whose Lectures she attended, and likewise from the professors of Anatomy and Practice of Physick in that City." The few men who began to advertise themselves as "man-midwives" did not present serious competition to women during the eighteenth century. As a correspondent to the *Virginia Gazette* observed, "A long unimpassioned Practice, early commenced, and calmly pursued is absolutely requisite to give Men by Art, what Women attain by Nature."

Because of the absence of formal educational requirements, a good many women were also able to enter the teaching profession. Some of these were governesses who lived with the family while educating the children. They commonly taught reading, writing, arithmetic, French, music, and needlework. Others opened schools of their own. Often a school was a family business in which husband and wife offered to teach different subjects.

The legal profession was technically closed to women and none appear as judges in colonial America. Since training for lawyers was very informal, however, some women did become proficient in conducting legal business. Most women who managed large farms or substantial business did their own legal work. They often held power of attorney to act for male relatives. Women might draft wills and other legal documents, and a few served as notaries. Usually colonial courts named the wife as executor of her husband's estate if he died without leaving a will.

The established churches did not recognize women as priests or ministers, and in fact Anne Hutchinson was banished from Massachusetts for even attempting to teach the Bible in private meetings. Yet many of the American sects did not have ordained clergy, and here women could freely participate. The Quakers had women preachers from the earliest period. The Moravians had women elders. Ann Lee, founder of the Shakers, and Jemimah Wilkinson, who was known as the Universal Friend, established religious communities of their own.

The true extent of economic opportunity available to eighteenth-century women is measured not by the small number of women in the professions, but by the ease with which women could establish themselves in business as independent agents. Even widows and spinsters with no family business to fall back on managed to establish themselves in some sort of profitable occupation.

The extent of women's involvement in the economic activities of their communities clearly demonstrates that there was no notion of a confined sphere of proper feminine activity in colonial America. It never occurred to anyone that a woman compromised her femininity if she demonstrated competence in what were later defined as "masculine" skills. Whatever English lawbooks might say, and whatever English moralists might preach, American women of the Revolutionary era gloried in their strength and independence. Later, in the nineteenth century, it was inconceivable for a notice such as the following to appear in an American newspaper: "John Cantwell has the impudence to advertise me in the Papers, cautioning all Persons against crediting me; he never had any Credit till he married me: As for his Bed and Board mention'd, he had neither Bed nor Board when he married me; I never eloped, I went away before his Face when he beat me." The confidence that colonial women could have in their ability to support themselves without a husband produced a generation of women with a degree of self-respect that later generations would view as brazen, unfeminine, and unladylike.

3

WOMEN'S ROLE
AND WOMEN'S RIGHTS

The concept of women's rights and status that the first English settlers brought to America was unusually liberal. England was ruled by a great queen, Elizabeth I, at the time the English made their first tentative approaches to the North American continent. The first permanent settlement was made in Virginia, a colony named in her honor. Anne Bradstreet, the New England poet, called up the memory of the famous queen in defending women against the charge that their minds were not equal to those of men:

> *Now say, have women worth? Or have they none?*
> *Or had they some, but with our Queen is't gone?*

Nay Masculines, you have thus taxt us long,
But she, though dead, will vindicate our wrong.
Let such as say our Sex is void of Reason,
Know tis a Slander now, but once was Treason.

Elizabeth, however, was not the only powerful woman in late sixteenth-century England. Other women of the upper classes could and did hold courts, vote for members of Parliament, exercise the privileges of knights of the kingdom, and participate vigorously in the religious and political conflicts of the day. When the common law of England threatened to limit the independence and property rights of females of aristocratic families, ways were found to keep their prerogatives intact by applying to courts of equity. Lower-class women, like lower-class men, had few rights of any sort. Nevertheless, sex was not a barrier to most occupations in sixteenth- and seventeenth-century England. In particular the right of women to belong to the trade guilds that preserved monopolies in certain enterprises for their members was well established. So was their right to assume the legal status known as "feme sole trader" which permitted them to carry on business activities independently of their husbands.

In England women began to lose some of their rights during the seventeenth century. But in America the pioneer conditions encouraged a further extension of women's rights. Furthermore, in the colonies, poor women as well as the rich benefited from gradual modifications of the common law. When it was strictly interpreted, as it would be in America in the nineteenth century, the common law was very unkind to women. It was especially unkind to married women. Under the common law a woman was considered legally dead once she married. She ceased to exist because marriage made her one person with her husband and he was that person. She could not be a witness in court, control her earnings, choose where she would live, or control her property. Her husband was legally entitled to beat her if she disobeyed him. She herself was the property of her husband. He could hire her out as a servant to anyone he chose and pocket her wages. If she ran away from him with the clothes she was wearing she might be considered a thief for stealing herself and the clothing, for both belonged to her husband. Colonial court records, however, show that the common law was not enforced consistently. Especially in the period before 1750, there were few trained lawyers in America, and wives were permitted to do many things which, strictly speaking, were illegal.

The common law was somewhat kinder to unmarried women — spinsters and widows. Theoretically they could not be forced to marry without their consent. They could own and manage any property they could acquire through inheritance or their own labor. Especially in the early years of colonization a woman of property could acquire as much social and political power as a man — so long as she did not take a husband. This freedom, however, was of little value to women without property. Widows could generally claim only one third of their husband's property. (The remainder went to the state, children, or other relatives depending on the circumstances.) If this was not enough to keep them from poverty they would be subject to the poor laws. Those laws prescribed compulsory labor so that impoverished widows might be bound out to serve as domestics. In Wareham, Massachusetts, there was an annual auction of indigent widows. Unless a widow was extremely poor or extremely old, however, she was not likely to remain unmarried very long.

There was great social pressure on both men and women in colonial America to marry. A Virginian boasting of America's advantages declared that "an Old Maid or an Old Bachelor are as scarce among us and reckoned as ominous as a Blazing Star." Men without families were thought to be evading their responsibilities to society. Unless he had a wife and children a man could not expect to contribute to the economic growth of the community. He could not rise to a position of prestige. A woman who refused to marry was viewed with horror and contempt. The religious beliefs of the colonists encouraged them to consider marriage a holy institution, which was the whole end of women's existence. Woman was created to be a helpmate to her husband. She had no other purpose in God's scheme. A woman without a husband and children was an unnatural creature. It was assumed that every woman wanted a husband and any female who said she did not was assumed to be lying to conceal the fact that she was unable to find a man who would have her. The "old maid" was depicted in literature as homely, bad-tempered, and eaten up with jealousy of married women. In 1790 a North Carolina newspaper described her as "one of the most cranky, ill-natured, maggotty, peevish, conceited, disagreeable, hypocritical, fretful, noisy, gibing, canting, censorious, out-of-the-way, never-to-be-pleased, good for nothing creatures . . . Of all things on earth she says she hates a man, because every man hates her . . . In short, an old maid enters the world to take up room, not to make room for others." Given such attitudes in society it is no wonder that few women voluntarily chose to remain single. In 1764 a Georgia newspaper carried the report of the death of an "old-virgin" who at the age of one hundred and nine had still been hoping to find a husband. Her search had probably lasted for nearly a century.

Men and women of the lower classes married at later ages than those of more prosperous families. A certain amount of property was necessary to set up an independent household. Unless one of the parties to the marriage had inherited some property, they must put off the wedding until one of them could earn enough. Yet when money was not a problem, it was natural for young girls to begin thinking of husbands at a very early age. Alice Lee, a twelve-year-old Virginia heiress, had a great desire to enter "the holy sacred institution" and grew angry at a relative for "retarding her success in the Matrimonial Way." Early in the eighteenth century it was reported of North Carolina, "They marry very young; some at thirteen or fourteen; and she that stays till twenty is reckoned a stale maid, which is a very indifferent character in that warm country." Daughters of wealthy families were usually given their share of the family fortune when they came of age or when they married, whichever arrived first. Marriage very commonly did come before they were out of their teens. Even among middle-class women, failure to marry by the age of twenty-five was considered a humiliation.

Because of the high death rate in eighteenth-century America, finding one husband did not assure a woman that she would remain a wife for the rest of her life. A widow, particularly if she had property, was expected to find a second husband with all due speed. If she had no property, of course, she would have to find a husband to support her. There had even been an attempt in Maryland early in the seventeenth century to order the confiscation of any property held by a woman unless she married within seven years. Yet there was no need for such coercive measures. Single life for both sexes was physically and psychologically difficult. Widows with property were very popular and usually took a new husband before the first had been buried a year. George Washington won the person and the fortune of Mrs. Martha Custis and married her barely seven months after the death of her first husband. This action showed no unusual haste. It was not unknown for widows to remarry within a few weeks or even a few days after their first husband died. Widowers remarried with equal haste. If the second marriage was ended by the death of the husband, the widow was not discouraged and looked for a third spouse.

Widows and widowers remained in the marriage market all their lives, and if necessary might take four, five, or even six marriage partners. Since marriage was supposed to be based on practical considerations rather than "passion," those who had already been married one or more times were often considered more suitable partners than young people were. Thus, in North Carolina, a gentleman about seventy, who was described as a "hearty Methuselah" married an "antiquated widow" of about forty-five, who, although she was "old-fashioned, ugly, and horribly formal" was also an excellent nurse. A young man, with less need of nursing, might find an elderly widow with a suitable inheritance from former husbands, an entirely appropriate match. Thus we read the following announcement in the *Virginia Gazette* for March 15, 1771: "Yesterday was married, in Henrico, Mr. William Carter, third son of Mr. John Carter, aged twenty-three, to Mrs. Sarah Ellyson, Relict of Mr.

Gerard Ellyson deceased, aged eighty-five, a sprightly old
Tit, with three Thousand Pounds Fortune." No wonder
young girls fearful of becoming old maids worried about
such competition! The *South Carolina Gazette* printed a
petition of unmarried women in which they declared
they were "in a very melancholy Disposition of mind,
considering how all the Bachelors are blindly captivated
by Widows." They asked that the governor intervene to
prevent any young man from marrying a widow until all
the unmarried women had had at least one chance.

Women who had any property before they married
usually made a premarriage contract with their prospective husbands. In this way the total control that the
common law would give the husband was somewhat
limited. And, of course, in a good marriage, where
affection if not deep love developed between the partners,
the provisions of the law were unimportant. A man who
was fond of his wife would want to be her friend, not her
master. Unfortunately, there is evidence of a great many
marriages that were not good. Marriage was contracted
for life, and since the two parties could not escape each
other their relationship might easily progress from indifference to each other, to irritation, to hatred, and finally
to physical cruelty and even attempted murder. When
the marriage turned into a war, many wives gave as good
as they got. John Custis of Virginia and his wife Frances
Parke Custis fought constantly except for those periods
when they refused to speak to each other at all and

communicated through their servants. At one point they tried to establish a truce and signed a formal contract in which each promised not to call the other "vile names," to "live lovingly together" and to "behave themselves to each other as a good husband & wife ought to do." Mrs. Custis agreed not to meddle with her husband's business affairs and he promised not to meddle with her running of the house and to give her half his income each year. This document did not "end all animositys and unkindness" between the two. Peace came only with Mrs. Custis's death. On his tombstone John Custis ordered these words carved: "Aged 71 Years, and yet lived but seven years, which was the space of time he kept a bachelor's home at Arlington on the Eastern Shore of Virginia."

Usually, however, the greater physical strength of the husband and the support his insistence on having his way got from the common law, made the wife the loser in domestic conflicts. Many women were made miserable by unfaithful husbands. Adultery by a wife was considered a grievous offense, but it was considered natural for a man to sin in that way from time to time. A man had grounds for divorce if his wife took another lover. But a woman was expected to tolerate her husband's mistresses. Indeed, if she should uncover his affairs and make a scene about them, he would be justified in leaving her. Women were told that they should not be upset by a husband's unfaithfulness, but those who cared for their husbands were heartbroken and humiliated. Society approved of a

moderate amount of wife-beating. Since the law made
the husband responsible for his wife's conduct, it was felt
proper that he should be able to discipline her if she
misbehaved herself. Unless she was permanently crippled
by the blows, the law considered the beating to be
"moderate punishment" and so permissible. Some men,
however, practiced cruelty toward their wives that clearly
exceeded what was lawful. Governor Dinwiddie of
Virginia reported a clergyman to the Bishop of London,
declaring that he had almost killed his wife by "ty'g her
up by the Leggs to the Bed Post and cut'g her in a cruel
Man'r with Knives." A Virginia man searched desper-
ately for some legal relief for a female relative whose
husband's cruelty had "already occasioned her to make
two or three attempts to destroy herself which if not
timely prevented will inevitably follow."

The law, however, was rarely of any help in such
situations. The courts in New England rarely and in the
South never granted absolute divorces before the Revolution. Marriages were to endure so long as both parties
lived. Understandably the deaths that dissolved an
unhappy union were not always natural. In Maryland
one John Steadman was executed for the murder of his
wife whose bruised body had been discovered in her bed
with the marks of a man's fingers on her throat. A few
years later another Maryland man was apprehended after
shooting his wife while she was asleep. In South Carolina
it was reported that a man "living unhappy with his

wife," committed suicide. Wives who were tempted to murder their husbands would discover that the law would again place them at a disadvantage if they succumbed to the impulse. A man who murdered his wife would be hanged. But a woman who murdered her husband was guilty of petty treason, just like a slave who murdered a master, and the penalty for petty treason was burning alive.

The best solution for a woman who found herself in an intolerable marriage was to run away. Running away was not legal. A wife had no more right to leave her husband's home than had one of his slaves or servants. If she did go off, he often advertised for her in the newspaper just as he would for a fugitive slave. Indeed, the newspapers in the Southern colonies contained almost equal numbers of ads for runaway wives and runaway slaves. Thus the *South Carolina Gazette* carried the following notice in May, 1765: "Whereas my wife Mary Oxendine, hath eloped from me, this is to forewarn all persons from Harbouring or entertaining her, day or night, or crediting her in my name, as I am determined not to pay any debts by her contracted. All masters of vessels or others, are hereby cautioned against carrying her off the province, as they may expect to be prosecuted with the utmost severeity. — She is of fair complexion, with light colour'd hair, and has a mark over one of her eyes."

Whatever the law might say, however, wives in

eighteenth-century America were not so helpless as slaves. The custom of the country tolerated women refusing to live with men if they found the connection unbearable. Women had the skills and opportunity to support themselves in a variety of occupations and they came to consider abandonment of husbands to be their right. When a man had advertised his wife as a runaway, he sometimes read a spirited reply to himself in the next issue. Thus Margaret Franks of South Carolina informed the public of the "true state" of her "supposed elopement" from her husband. "My now being absent from him," she told the readers of the *South Carolina Gazette*, "was occasioned by his most cruel and inhuman Treatment to me, . . . by his severe Threats, Blows, and turning me out of Doors, in the Dead of Night, leaving me, and a poor helpless inflant, whom I had by a former Husband, naked, and exposed to the inclemency of the Wather." Another woman declared that she had left home because of her husband's "inhumanity and preferring an old negro wench for a bedfellow."

Although the courts would not grant absolute divorces, which would have permitted the parties to remarry, they did occasionally approve of a woman living apart from her husband and would order him to support her. Such an order might be issued if the wife could prove such extreme cruelty that her life was in danger. In practice, however, married couples in some parts of the country were able to practice divorce by mutual consent by means of wholly illegal contracts that were nonetheless recognized by the community. In North and South Carolina, Virginia, and Maryland, couples who wished to separate drew up agreements by which they divided their property and promised never to claim each other as husband and wife in the future. These agreements were published in the newspapers. Although no court would have regarded them as binding, the individuals involved considered themselves freed from their marriage vows and commonly remarried. Settlers on the frontier sometimes abandoned European views of marriage entirely and began to form relationships on the Indian pattern. In the absence of churches and clergymen, young people might have to wait for the appearance of an itinerant preacher before they could have a marriage ceremony. The religious credentials of the preacher were often questionable and he sometimes did not appear until the young couple had a child or two to be baptised after the marriage service was completed. It is not surprising that couples married in this way did not consider their vows indissolvable. They separated and formed new marriages simply by mutual consent. Missionaires into the back country were horrified to see white people exercising such unrestrained sexual freedom, "Swapping away their Wives and Children, as they would Horses or Cattle" as a complaint to the South Carolina Assembly put it.

At the time of the Revolution, then, lower-class and middle-class women could enjoy substantial sexual freedom. They could choose to ignore both church law and common law regulations. They did not care whether members of the upper classes found their behavior shocking. The courts would not interfere unless "illegitimate" children were abandoned and became a burden on the community or the couple living "in sin" behaved in a way that disturbed the neighbors. Upper-class women, however, could not escape from a burdensome marriage so easily. A husband who was a man of wealth and position would be able to hire lawyers and enforce his legal rights. If she did anything as disgraceful as running away she would certainly lose all claim to her property and to her children. Finally, the strong sense of class that existed in revolutionary America made it impossible for a woman of "the better sort" to adopt the behavior patterns of lower-class women. Such a woman would feel deep humiliation if she did anything "unladylike."

There were relatively few "ladies" in America at the time of the Revolution. In the early years of settlement there was not enough wealth or leisure for either men or women to allow time to cultivate elegant manners or encourage imitation of the life style of European aristocrats. Toward the middle of the eighteenth century a small class of wealthy merchants, landowners, and government officials developed on the seaboard, especially in the cities, which began to look toward the English court for role models. They were not really aristocrats as that term was understood in Europe, but they wanted to be.

The women looked for ways to cultivate refined manners and tried to imitate the clothing styles that would mark them as clearly different from their social inferiors. In seeking equality with the aristocratic women of England, however, they were forced to give up much of the social, sexual, political, and economic freedom enjoyed by ordinary American women.

When a woman of the upper class was caught in an unhappy marriage she looked for solutions in the manuals of social conduct that set down the principles by which ladies were expected to guide their lives. Before the middle of the eighteenth century women read the Bible and other devotional literature, cookbooks and medical texts, and after that the same body of political, historical, or philosophical literature that men read. In the eighteenth century, upper-class women began to read what were known as "ladies' books." They had such titles as *The Ladies Calling*, *The Ladies Library*, and *The Lady's New Years Gift*, and they told women how they must behave if they wanted to be considered refined and genteel. The books were written in England (almost all of them by men), and some of them had been popular among English ladies for almost a century before they began to attract any attention in America. Two new books that appeared just before the Revolution, Dr. Gregory's *A Father's Legacy to his Daughters* and Dr. Fordyce's *Sermons to Young Women*, became extremely popular among the small class of American ladies. If their aim was to find patterns of behavior that would set them off from ordinary American women they could hardly have found better models. Both Dr. Gregory and Dr. Fordyce urged the ladies to cultivate passive and negative qualities. Women must never be outstanding in anything. Even a robust constitution might be considered "masculine." Thus Dr. Gregory warned, "Though good health be one of the greatest blessings of life, never make a boast of it; but enjoy it in grateful silence. We [men] so naturally associate the idea of female softness and delicacy with a correspondent delicacy of constitution, that when a woman speaks of her great strength, her extraordinary appetite, her ability to bear excessive fatigue, we recoil at the description, in a way she is little aware of." Their advice to ladies who wanted to be happy with their husbands was to surrender their wills completely to their husbands and be totally submissive and obedient to his commands.

Obedience to a husband was a wife's duty first, because she promised it as part of the marriage ceremony and second, because it was God's will. According to the ministers who wrote ladies' books, the sin of Eve in the Garden of Eden was punished by putting women for ever after under the domination of men. It was worse than useless, it was impious for a woman to resist this natural order. Although it is uncertain just how many women tried to live up to this goal before the Revolution, those who instructed young women were unanimous in recommending it as the only hope for happiness. For example, Dr. Benjamin Rush, who is considered liberal in his views on women because he favored women's education, advised a young lady about to be wed, "Don't be offended when I add that from the day you marry you must have no will of your own. The subordination of your sex to ours is enforced by nature, by reason, and by revelation . . . In no situation whatever, let the words 'I will' or 'I won't' fall from your lips till you have first found out your husband's inclinations in a matter that interests you both. The happiest marriages I have known have been those when the subordination I have recommended has been most complete." Some women certainly tried to achieve this ideal which, of course, would have been easier with some men than with others. Henry Laurens was completely satisfied with his wife. He mourned the death of the woman he described as his "bosom friend," declaring she was "ever loving, cherishing and ready to obey — who never once, — no, not *once* — during the course of twenty years' most intimate connection threw the stumbling block of opposition" against his desires.

The ladies' books agreed that even when a wife was totally submissive and obedient she could not expect to find love in her marriage. Indeed, most said she ought not to want love. Certainly she must never give the slightest hint to a suitor that she was fond of him. George Washington advised his stepdaughter that the first move, "without the *most indirect* invitation of yours, must proceed from the man to render it permanent and valuable." When he proposed, good form required that she pretend to be displeased and only accept him after he has been kept waiting as long as possible and asked her several times. Dr. Gregory said it was not "consistent with the perfection of female delicacy" to admit she was in love. If a married woman should have some affection for her husband she was warned not to admit it because such a confession would fill her husband with "satiety and disgust." Another writer warned married women against expressing any affection for her husband in public or annoying him by complaining of missing him when he was away. Dr. Gregory explained what love should be for a lady: "Some agreeable qualities recommend a gentleman to your good liking and friendship. In the course of his acquaintance he contracts an attachment to you. When you perceive it, it excites your gratitude; this gratitude rises into preference; and this preference, perhaps, at least advances to some degree of attachment . . . If attachment was not excited in your sex in this manner, there is not one of a million of you that could ever marry with any degree of love." At any rate, the writers generally agreed that once a man possessed a woman by marrying her he would soon cease to love her very deeply. The best she could hope for was to build the foundation of friendship while his passion was cooling.

This advice may have made sense to English ladies of

the eighteenth century, but even upper-class women of eighteenth-century America could not have felt it mirrored their experience. As the ladylike ideal became established in the nineteenth century, women became more reticent about their sexual feelings. But in the eighteenth century, even in Puritan New England, men and women frankly acknowledged that they aroused each other. John Adams wrote to his future wife while they were courting, "Every experimental Phylosopher knows, that the steel and the Magnet or the Glass and feather will not fly together with more Celerity, than somebody and somebody, when brought within striking Distance." Of course, this letter was written more than a decade before the Revolution. When John and Abigail's children were grown and attempted to contract marriages on the basis of love, the parents intervened and insisted that the younger generation follow their heads rather than their hearts.

The ladies' books' injunction against refined women participating in political activity was also impossible for American women to accept in the eighteenth century. Dr. Fordyce's explanations seemed difficult to apply in the American context: "War, commerce, politics, exercises of strength and dexterity, abstract philosophy, and all the abstrusser sciences, are most propertly the province of men . . . those masculine women that would plead for your sharing any part of this province equally with us, do not understand your true interests. There is an influence, there is an empire which belongs to you, and which I wish you ever to possess: I mean that which has the heart for its object and is secured by meekness, by soft attraction, and virtuous love." American women who were anxious to become ladies might worry about having political interests, but at the time of the Revolution they found that their husbands welcomed such interest. Even the most fastidious lady decided, if she had any inclination toward politics, that so long as her politics were of the right sort so that they did not cause arguments with her husband and so long as she did not let her political interests interfere with her domestic duties, she might allow herself to be a politician. From a husband's point of view, it was comforting to realize that a woman who was a serious student of politics would not become a flighty, frivolous, good-for-nothing lady of fashion. And fashionable ladies were considered as dangerous as disobedient wives.

The wealthy women of America who searched for role models in the middle of the eighteenth century were faced with a dilemma. They were told not to imitate the great ladies of the Elizabethan period who were bold and aggressive and often outdid their husbands in their conduct of political and sexual intrigues. On the other hand, ladies of eighteenth-century England who spent their time on unproductive activities and spent vast sums of money keeping up with the latest fashions were too great a luxury even for the wealthiest colonists. When colonial newspapers discussed the problems of married life, the extravagance of women was often cited as the chief problem. As the lady of fashion became the ideal in England, the clothing worn by upper-class women became increasingly more elaborate, more uncomfortable, and more expensive. Shortly before the Revolution engraved fashion plates illustrating the latest mode in London began to be popular in the colonies and the upper classes began to adopt as much as they could afford. Large hoop petticoats, stiff stays, and elaborate high hairdos were adopted by those who wished to appear aristocratic. Men had difficulty understanding why women wished to adopt these styles. In 1773 a Virginia man described a young lady named Elizabeth Lee: "She was pinched up rather too near in a long pair of new fashioned Stays, which, I think, are a Nuisance both to us & themselves. For the late importation of stays which are said to be now most fashionable in London, are produced upwards so high that we can have scarce any view at all of the Ladies Snowy Bosoms; & on the contrary, they are extended downwards so low that whenever Ladies who wear them, either young or old have occasion to walk, the motion necessary for Walking must, I think cause a disagreeable Friction of some part of the body against the lower Edge of the Stays which is hard & unyielding. I imputed the Flush which was visible in her Face to her being swathed by Body & Soul & Limbs together."

The cost of the items necessary to the wardrobe of a

lady of fashion made it necessary to abandon the attempt to acquire them during the Revolutionary crisis. Although the desire to look like an English aristocrat was clearly growing on the eve of the conflict, it was impossible for American men to encourage their wives to purchase unnecessary luxury items from the enemy. Indeed ladies of fashion found themselves the target of vigorous attack both for wasting money and for failing to concentrate their attention and their energies on the serious problems facing the country. Upper-class women who had been flirting with the idea of adopting the English ideal generally gave up the effort for the duration of the war. The women who read the ladies' books and thought of themselves as aristocrats were a minority of American women. Another minority at the other end of the social scale was made up of servant women.

There was no sharp line between free women and women in economic bondage during the colonial period. Husbands, after all, had the right to sell the services of their wives and collect their wages. Furthermore, although marriage was supposed to be a matter of free choice, the conditions under which many women came to the colonies made real freedom of choice impossible. Many unmarried women came in shiploads to the colonies in the seventeenth and eighteenth centuries expecting to find a husband to pay their passage money as soon as they landed. When women were scarce, the captain of a bride ship might demand more than passage money and auction off the women for whatever price the market would bear. (Theoretically the women could refuse to honor the bargain.)

The sale of wives was practiced openly in England right into the eighteenth century. In America, however, it seems to have been a rare occurrence and not generally approved. A New York man was sentenced to be flogged and have an ear cut off when he tried to sell his wife in 1663. Some years earlier a man in Hartford, Connecticut, was fined for attempting to leave his wife to another man by a provision in his will. And yet, as late as 1736, a Boston newspaper reported an incident in which one man sold his wife to another for the sum of fifteen shillings — the price of half a pound of tea. Whether or not the wife was pleased with the arrangement is not recorded. Certainly the distinction between a purchased bride and a bondservant is indistinct.

Women who did not find husbands as soon as they landed would probably be sold as indentured servants. Their masters would own their labor for a stated period of time in return for paying the passage money. If the master wished he could sell his servant just as he could a slave. Advertisements like the following are found in colonial papers alongside ads offering black slaves for sale: "To be sold An Irish Servant girl's time, being 4 years and 3 months; she is fit for either town or country and is a very good spinster." Or, "A likely young Dutch servant woman's time for three years to be disposed of, she is a very good seamstress at Extraordinary or plain work, and pretty handy at house work; those inclined to purchase her time many agree with Anthony Furnas in Philadelphia." The treatment a servant girl received depended on her owners. Some were kind and generous, taught their servants and slaves to read, fed them well and did not overwork them. But there is also evidence of cruelty to servants. An English girl who was sold to a family in Maryland wrote to her father in 1756, "I . . . am toiling almost Day and Night . . . and then tied up and whipp'd to that Degree that you'd not serve an Annimal, scarce any thing but Indian Corn and Salt to eat and that even begrudged nay many Neagroes are better used, almost naked no shoes nor stockings to wear, and the comfort after slaving dureing Masters pleasure, what rest can get is to rap ourselves up in a Blanket and ly upon the Ground, this is the deplorable Conditions you poor Betty endures." Unlike the black slave, a servant who felt ill-treated was legally entitled to sue in the courts. But this action took great courage. If the suit was lost the servant was sure to be beaten.

One of the special hardships faced by servant girls was their inability to marry without the consent of their owners. If she married without his consent she would be forced to serve an extra year for him. If she ran away with her prospective husband and was caught she might be whipped and have her time in service doubled. If she became pregnant out of wedlock, her master would have to pay a fine to assure that the illegitimate child would not become a public charge, and the mother would, again, have to serve extra time to reimburse him. Some masters deliberately got their own servant girls pregnant in order to force them to serve extra time. In addition, mothers (but not fathers) of illigitimate children were publicly whipped. The result of this severity did not decrease the number of illegitimate children born, but encouraged both abortion and infanticide.

Nevertheless, however hard the life of a serving woman might be, she could be comforted to know that her bondage would not last forever. Most white servants served out their terms and found a free man to marry. There is every reason to believe that most of them ended up as free as any woman could be in the eighteenth century.

4

BLACK WOMEN

ALTHOUGH almost all of them were slaves, the status of black women in eighteenth-century America was higher than it would be in the next century. Status is a relative concept. It implies comparison with the status of others. In the eighteenth century, the approximately twenty percent of the population that was enslaved was deprived of the right to choose employers freely, could not marry without a master's consent, was forced to obey rules of conduct set down by the master and could be beaten for disobedience, and, of course, was deprived of the right to vote. But these restrictions applied to most people in the eighteenth century. Wives, indentured servants, appren-

tices, and children under twenty-one were also legally
bound to obey the male head of the household and could
be beaten or otherwise punished for violating his commands. Similarly, most of the black population wore
coarse clothing, lived in one room shacks, and never
tasted white bread or Madeira wine. But the same was
true of most of the white population. In the nineteenth
century as the legal rights of white males were extended,
as their economic opportunities expanded, and as the
standard of living of all whites improved, the *relative*
status of blacks declined. For black *women*, the decline
was, perhaps, not so great as for the race as a whole. In
the eighteenth century, the status of black women was
lower than that of black men and lower than that of white
women. In the nineteenth century, the status of black
men was not raised and that of white women was
lowered.

One great distinction that was made between white
and black women throughout the period of slavery was
that black women worked in the fields while white
women ordinarily did not. As early as 1656, it was a set
policy in the colonies that white servant women would be
put to work as domestics. Only those "wenches that are
nasty, and beastly and not fit to be so employed are put
into the ground." There was no doubt in the mind of the
early colonists that only black women fell into that
category. The special character of black women's labor
was emphasized by the tax laws of early Virginia. All

productive — that is agricultural — laborers were taxed. White women were not taxed, but a tax was levied on all black women both slave and free. The clear presumption was that black women worked in the fields.

Slavery was not confined to the South before the Revolution. Substantial numbers of slaves were found in the middle colonies — especially New York — and even in New England. In those areas most farms were small and slaves were not worked in gangs. Black women were used largely to assist the woman of the house with "women's work." Furthermore, even southern plantations had not yet experienced the agricultural revolution that brought large-scale cotton and sugar production to the South in the nineteenth century. Here, too, the women were somewhat less likely to be worked in gangs with men than they were in the nineteenth century. In all parts of the country, however, black women were required to do field work in colonial times. On large units, men did the plowing, but on smaller units a good number of slave women were used for that heavy work. Some individual women were stronger than most men, and it was not infrequent for a planter to note that the most valuable field hand on his place was a woman. Individual black women matched the men not only in plowing but in other physically demanding work, such as rolling logs and chopping wood. Considering the work white frontier women were capable of, this is hardly surprising.

Field work was an unskilled, low-status occupation.
The use of women slaves in that work depressed their
status not merely relative to white women but relative to
black men as well. There were other occupations open to
blacks, even to black slaves, in the colonial period, but
men were far more likely than women to have the
opportunity to enter them. Slaves who came to America
fresh from Africa, who could not speak English and who
were not accustomed to white ways, were of limited use
to their owners. They were valuable only for their
muscles. But as time went on, a good number of slaves
were trained in a skill. Their owners could then use them
as domestic servants, blacksmiths, weavers, carpenters,
and so forth on the plantation, or could hire them out to
work for others. A slave who had been trained in a skill
had higher status in his master's eyes and in the eyes of
the slave community. He was given greater independence in his work, and his skill often enabled him to earn
money of his own in his free time. Money, in turn,
might make it possible for the slave to purchase himself
and perhaps his wife and children as well.

Unfortunately, slave women were far less likely than
slave men to be trained in marketable skills. Virtually the
only escape from the fields was in domestic service.
Women might be cooks, body servants, nurses, or they
might spin, sew, or care for children. Except for the job
of chief cook or plantation "Mammy," there were no
supervisory jobs open to women slaves. Perhaps the

majority of women who did get work in the house were put to domestic activity because they were too old to work any longer in the fields.

Free black women, particularly in the North, might do somewhat better. Dutchess Quamino ran a successful catering business in Newport, Rhode Island. Catherine Ferguson of New York, who had purchased her own freedom, established "Katy Ferguson's School for the Poor" in 1793 and taught both black and white children. The federal census of 1790 and the tax lists of various cities reveal a substantial number of free black women named as "head of family" and owning enough property to be assessed for taxes. Freedom did not solve all problems faced by black women in the colonial period, but it did restore near equality with black men.

The prejudice that white colonists felt against blacks was nowhere more starkly revealed than in the laws forbidding interracial marriage. All of the southern colonies, Massachusetts, and Pennsylvania had laws against sexual union of black and white. Under these laws persons of mixed blood, who might to all appearances be white, were considered to be black. There were black men and white women and white men and black women who set up households and raised families in spite of the law. But these "marriages" were not considered legitimate. Furthermore, Americans considered an extramarital relationship particularly reprehensible if it involved members of two races. Individuals of both sexes and both races suffered private tragedies because of these laws. Black women, however, suffered most. While white women might inherit some wealth and status from their fathers and had opportunities to improve their economic condition through their own work, a black woman could achieve a life of ease and comfort only by becoming the mistress of a prosperous white man. Furthermore, no matter how kind the man might be, though he might buy her expensive clothes and provide freedom and property for her in his will, a black mistress could never be the equal of a white wife. She was often despised by both races and could never forget that if she lost her man's favor or angered his relatives she and her children might be separated and sold at any moment.

Society was most tolerant of black mistresses in the West Indies. On the American continent tolerance of black-white relationships decreased the farther north one proceeded. A gentleman from Jamaica wrote from Charleston in 1773, "I know of but one Gentleman who professedly keeps a Mulatto Mistress and he is very much pointed at: There are swarms of Negroes about the Town and many Mulattoes, and by the Dress of the Girls, who mostly imitate their Mistresses, I have no doubt of their Conversations with the whites, but they are carried on with more privacy than in our W. India Islands . . . As I travell'd further North [to North Carolina] there were fewer Negroes about the Houses, and these taken less notice of, and before I finish'd my

Journey North, I found an empty House, the late Tenant of which had been oblig'd by the Church Wardens to decamp on Account of his having kept a Black Woman." A French visitor to America cited as an example of racial prejudice the unwillingness of Americans to rent houses to "colored prostitutes." Although colonial Americans did not approve of fornication, they were far more tolerant of it than Americans of the nineteenth century. Yet interracial sex was regarded with horror.

The story of Sally Hemings and Thomas Jefferson, which has been told and retold since the early years of the nineteenth century, reveals more about the racial attitudes of white Americans than it does about the private lives of either of the individuals involved. The woman who has been exploited by scandalmongers as "Black Sal," was not, in fact, very black. A man like Jefferson, who accepted European rather than African standards of feminine beauty, would have seen nothing alien in her appearance. Her mother, Elizabeth Hemings, was a mulatto with a white father. Sally's father was probably John Wayles, Jefferson's father-in-law. Sally herself was light-skinned. She was described by one who knew her as "very handsome: long straight hair down her back." When John Wayles died, Elizabeth Hemings and her children became Jefferson's property. Jefferson's wife, Martha, who probably was Sally's half-sister, died in 1782. Five years later, when Sally was about fifteen, she went to France with Jefferson and his younger daughter,

Polly. They remained abroad for a year and a half. Sally's son Madison described what happened then in these words: "During that time my mother became Mr. Jefferson's concubine . . . He desired to bring my mother back to Virginia with him but she demurred. She was just beginning to understand the French language well, and in France she was free, while if she returned to Virginia she would be re-enslaved. So she refused to return with him. To induce her to do so he promised her extraordinary privileges, and made a solemn pledge that her children should be freed at the age of twenty-one years. In consequence of his promises, on which she implicitly [relied], she returned with him to Virginia. Soon after their arrival, she gave birth to a child, of whom Thomas Jefferson was the father. It lived but a short time. She gave birth to four others, and Jefferson was the father of all of them . . . We all became free agreeably to the treaty entered into by our parents before we were born." Two of these children passed into the white community.

Although vigorously denied by Jefferson's white descendants and repudiated out-of-hand by white male historians who found miscegenation repugnant, this account is not implausible. Jefferson was with Sally nine months before the birth of each of the children. He never remarried and Sally had no husband. If they indeed formed an extramarital relationship, it was one that endured for thirty-eight years. Madison recalled his mother's responsibilities at Monticello: "It was her duty, all her life which I can remember, up to the time of father's death, to take care of his chamber and wardrobe, look after us children and do such light work as sewing, &c." There is no reason to feel she was exploited more than a lawful wife or that the relationship between herself and Jefferson did not contribute to the happiness of both parties.

The disgrace or the evil in the relationship lay not in the conduct of the two individuals involved but in the attitudes of the white community. The following vicious verse is typical of attacks on Jefferson:

> In glaring red, and chalky white,
> Let others beauty see;
> Me no such tawdry tints delight —
> No! black's the hue for me!
>
> Thick pouting lips! how sweet their grace!
> When passion fires to kiss them!
> Wide spreading over half the face,
> Impossible to miss them.
>
> Oh! Sally! hearken to my vows!
> Yield up thy sooty charms —
> My best belov'd! my more than spouse,
> Oh! take me to thy arms!

The allegation of a long stable alliance between a white widower and an unmarried black woman was thought to damage Jefferson's reputation. Yet when Jefferson's archenemy Alexander Hamilton, a married man who was himself illegitimate, confessed to an affair with a married woman, it did little more than raise a few eyebrows.

Sally Hemings, whose ancestry was mostly white and who had been educated with white girls in America and France, was far removed from most of the black women of colonial America. She could not have fit into the black slave community that provided emotional comfort and security for the great majority of slave women.

When the first black slaves were sold in America there was a great disproportion of men over women. Slaves were housed in barracks or in barn lofts. Family life was virtually impossible. By the middle of the eighteenth century, however, the numbers of male and female slaves became roughly equal. Slaveowners provided individual cabins for slave couples. The black population soon succeeded in creating a reasonably stable family and community life that was immensely supportive in dealing with the physical and emotional strains of slavery. Contrary to common opinion, the slaveowners encouraged the development of slave families, some because of their moral views and others because they discovered that slaves who were happy with their domestic arrangements worked harder and were easier to control.

The whites often asserted their belief that blacks were promiscuous, that they had no sense of sexual morality. They sought to justify the sexual exploitation of black women in the slave quarters and the separation of black husbands and wives by arguing that such things did not really bother the slaves. That was not true. The blacks had a moral code, but it was derived from Africa rather than from Europe.

Africans did not believe that sex was dirty, disgusting, or sinful. Nakedness was not shameful, sexual jokes were not improper, and there was no double standard to make behavior that was acceptable in a man unacceptable in a woman. They did not distinguish between love and marriage. Therefore they would not recognize involuntary "marriage" — however "legal" it might be, and divorce was easily accepted when a couple grew dissatisfied with their relationship. On the other hand, adultery was considered an extremely grave offense. Although the black slaves modified their African morality after they were brought to America, the blacks — especially the black women — continued to be far less self-conscious and guilt-ridden about their sexuality than the Europeans. It was no contradiction that they also valued their monogamous relationships and resented both rape and the breakup of their families.

History shows that human beings have a remarkable ability to make the best of things. The black population of colonial America worked to make their lives as good as possible under the circumstances. Despite the hardships and the exploitation they endured, they generally succeeded in seizing some pleasure and satisfaction from their lives. They did not become animals even when they were treated as such. They preserved their humanity. Slave mothers and fathers managed to make homes for their children in their humble cabins.

The living conditions of slaves differed widely from place to place. Housing generally improved toward the end of the eighteenth century, but cabins were smaller and flimsier than they would be in the nineteenth century. In fairness it must be remembered that the housing of many white families in the eighteenth century was just as bad. A slave described the quarters on a Maryland plantation thus: "In a single room were huddled, like cattle, ten or a dozen persons, men, women and children . . . There were neither bedsteads, nor furniture of any description. Our beds were collections of straw and old rags, thrown down in the corner and boxed in with boards; a single blanket the only covering. Our favorite way of sleeping, however, was on a plank, our heads raised on an old jacket and our feet toasting before the smouldering fire." An English traveler who spent a night in a "miserable shell" inhabited by an overseer and six slaves said "it was not lathed nor plaistered, neither ceiled nor lofted above . . . one window, but no glass in it, not even a brick chimney, and as it stood on blocks about a foot above the ground, the hogs lay constantly under the floor, which made it swarm with flies." George Washington housed his slaves in small shacks that could be moved to different parts of the plantation to follow the crop. A Polish visitor to Mount Vernon declared these buildings to be "far more miserable than the poorest of the cottages of our peasants." On the other hand, many masters were concerned about the housing of their slaves. They gave orders to build warm, snug cabins with wood floors and fireplaces. Travelers described the clustered cabins as looking like small villages.

Slave cabins were usually decently, although by no means lavishly, furnished according to the standards of the time. An inventory of a slave cabin in Virginia in 1697 recorded that it contained a bed, a few chairs, one iron kettle, one brass kettle, one iron pot, one pair of potracks, one pothook, one frying pan, and a beer barrel. The slaves did what they could to provide themselves with other items. They were especially anxious to acquire cooking and eating utensils. If they lived near the sea they would collect shells to use as spoons and dishes. Dried gourds could become bowls, jugs, and ladles.

Since the cabin was the master's property, slave women had relatively little interest in doing more to it than keeping it clean. They made little effort to decorate or acquire additional furniture. Similarly, they had little interest in the fabric arts that so engrossed the attention of white women. The master provided the family's clothing. He had it made up out of heavy, coarse cloth. He did not waste money on dye. Children of both sexes wore short dresses until they were about twelve. The men had shirts and trousers, the latter often made of leather. Women were given loose-fitting smocks that tied around the waist and a short waistcoat to wear on top. Toward the end of the eighteenth century some slave women began to make quilts, an art at which they would become very expert in the nineteenth century. They had no inclination, however, to spend their leisure time spinning, preparing dyes, or doing embroidery as the white women did.

If the slaves were less concerned with clothing than the white population was, they were more concerned with personal cleanliness. In the warm climate of Africa it was the custom among the population from which American slaves were drawn to bathe daily. West Africans thought that Europeans, who came from a cold climate and believed baths were unhealthy, were unbelievably filthy. The Europeans, on the other hand, thought the African custom was very peculiar. In America the slaves had difficulty maintaining the African standard of cleanliness, particularly in the winter. It was their habit, however, to clean themselves well to celebrate the weekend every week. Sunday was a special day not merely because it was the sabbath, but because it was the day of rest when the slaves belonged to themselves rather than to the master. Despite their indifference to work-day clothing they tried to acquire brightly colored "fine" clothing — ideally something passed on from the mistress — to wear on the weekend. The most important part of the weekend celebrations, however, involved eating well. A Hessian officer in America during the Revolution noted that cooking was low in the scale of values for white American women. "The people are very fond of luxury, especially the women," he wrote, "which fondness shows itself in their dress and in their houses. However, the way of living in regard to food is very poor. No German stomach can put up with it." An authority on the history of food has said, "Cooking is an art only where food is consistently plentiful. When shortages are part of everyday life, filling the stomach is the only art." Certainly there were few places in the world where cooking was an art in the eighteenth century. Even in those countries that had pretentions to culinary elegance, fine cooking was usually available only to the rich. As for English cooking, all Europeans seemed to agree that it was ghastly. In 1748 a Swede conceded that "Englishmen understand almost better than any other people the art of properly roasting a large cut of meet." But this, he said was "not to be wondered at; because the art of cooking as practiced by most Englishmen does not extend much beyond roast beef and plum pudding." In Africa, however, where the warm climate made food plentiful, cooking was indeed an art. Since the master was obliged to provide at least minimum rations for his slaves himself, blacks in America could confine their quest for food to extra luxury items and continue to cultivate their culinary traditions.

Slave owners provided their slaves with roughly the same kind of food lower-class whites ate. Corn was the staple. In addition the master might provide bacon and buttermilk. He also gave his slaves the pieces of meat he did not want for himself: the head, the feet, fatback, and innards. Such provisions would certainly keep a slave family from starving, but the blacks had higher standards. They made good use of what the master provided and supplemented their diet with what they could provide for themselves. Vegetables were easy. If the master did not allow the slaves to keep kitchen gardens of their own they could always steal from him. Meat was not much harder. The slaves were less willing than the white population to settle for salt meat. Stealing from the master and hunting could keep a black family in the South provided with fresh meat the year round.

It is no wonder that slaves felt no compunction about stealing from the master. They felt their work for him entitled them to eat well. If he did not provide enough they felt justified in taking what they could. The master, after all, had stolen human beings from themselves. How could it be wrong for those human beings to steal a few pigs from him? Furthermore, the wealthy planter had so many animals, how could he begrudge a few to his hungry servants? There certainly did seem to be an abundance of food on the Southern plantations. Pigs were not native to North America, but when the settlers introduced them in Virginia they multiplied rapidly. By the beginning of the eighteenth century they were so plentiful that William Byrd II declared that the people of Virginia themselves had become "extremely hoggish in their temper . . . and prone to grunt rather than speak." Nevertheless, stealing by slaves was so widespread that in 1748 Virginia decreed capital punishment for the third offense of pig-stealing. Plantation owner Robert Carter complained that stealing by slaves was making it unprofitable to farm in Virginia. When the slaves on a South Carolina plantation developed a taste for beef over pork, the plantation manager wrote to the owner to report on a wave of cattle thefts: "This kind of work prevails so much in your neighborhood that I fear few of your Creatures will be left by the year's end." Finally, a complaint from George Washington shows that the slave's search for a good dinner did not end with a joint of meat. Washington declared that out of every seven bottles of fine wine consumed on his plantation he drank only two; the slaves made off with the other five.

Slave men enjoyed hunting both for the sport and for the good dinner a successful expedition would produce. Since slaves generally did not own weapons, they hunted small game with dogs: rabbits, squirrels, raccoons, and above all opossum. The recipe for opossum remembered by nineteenth-century slaves was probably the same as that used earlier. Preparation of 'possum in a slave cabin involved parboiling the animal and then roasting it with lard or fatback surrounded by sweet potatoes.

Cooking held the place in the interest of black women that the fabric arts held for white women. In a life filled with hard work, they would exert themselves a little more to make the food they prepared something special. On weekends, when a friend or relative came to visit from a neighboring plantation, or when her husband caught or stole some special treat, a slave woman would bring all her skill to bear in preparing a memorable meal. The use of herbs and spices made black cooking distinctive. Red pepper, malaguetta pepper, and sesame seeds and oil came from Africa. Gumbos and jambalayas are examples of the subtly flavored dishes, entirely alien to European culinary traditions, that slaves introduced into America. Blacks also differed from the whites in their regard for "pot-likker." Both whites and blacks in the eighteenth century thought vegetables had to be boiled to the point of tastelessness before they were "done." But the whites compounded the problem by disgarding the water in which the vegetables were boiled, thus losing all the taste as well as all the vitamins. The black cooks, on the other hand, highly valued the liquid that the whites disdained.

Cooking was not a skill confined to black women. Both sexes enjoyed food and both were generally fine cooks. Boys and girls were both taught the art of preparing good things to eat. With so many talented cooks in the slave population, it is hardly surprising that black cuisine soon came to dominate in the kitchens of well-to-do whites. So-called "southern" cooking is the contribution of black slaves. They had more and better quality food to work with when they cooked for the white people, but the talent for cooking made even the humbler fare in the slave cabins tastier than what was eaten by most whites.

When the circumstances of slave life became unbearable, the only solution was to run away. Highly skilled slave artisans might run away in search of freedom and economic independence. Because masters regarded their slaves as valuable property, they were unlikely physically to abuse them, but slaves who had the bad luck to be purchased by mentally unbalanced individuals might flee from sadistic torture. The chief reason for running away, however, appears to have been to marry or to rejoin family members. Throughout the period of slavery the overwhelming majority of runaways were men. Fewer than 20 percent were women. Deprived of the training that would encourage economic ambitions, the women who ran away usually left to visit family or friends from whom they had been separated. Often these "runaways" came back to the plantation after they felt they had enjoyed an adequate visit. The breakup of family units and separation from friends—not physical hardship—appears to have been the most painful aspect of slavery. Masters could be astonishingly callous toward the personal attachments of slaves for each other. Consider the action of Charleston merchant Robert Pringle. He owned a slave girl named Esther. In 1740 he put her on a ship bound for Portugal with instructions to his agents there to try to "sell her to good Advantage." He declared "She is a Very likely Young Wench & can doe any House Work, such as Makeing Beds, Cleaning Rooms, Washing, Attending at Table &C. & talks good English being this Province Born, & is not given to any Vice." Furthermore, he had "always found her honest." His reason for sending her away was "that she had a practice of goeing frequently to her Father and Mother, who Live at a Plantation I am Concern'd in, about Twenty Miles from Town." As he found "there was no Refraining her from Running away there, & Staying every now & then," he was taking the extreme measure of putting an ocean between young Esther and her parents.

Separation from parents was always possible in slave life. As we have seen, however, children of white parents might also be sent from home at an early age. In some respects the life of slave children was easier than that of lower- and middle-class whites. They were rarely put to work before the age of ten. There were no whippings or punishments to "harden" them or "train their character," since the white people were not apt to think it worth their trouble to bring up slave children with the attention they gave their own. Often slave children were regarded like kittens or puppies and treated as pets. If the child grew up to be a field hand, adulthood would bring a sudden change in his treatment. House slaves, however, might be indulged and petted for a lifetime so long as they remained docile and friendly to their masters and mistresses. Young slaves were often purchased as companions for family children. It is not surprising that an affectionate relationship often grew up between them despite the barrier of slavery. Wills, especially in the Northern colonies, often included provisions freeing favored slaves and even providing them with an income. Phoebe Abdee was left her freedom and a hundred pounds a year by Abigail Adams' father. A gentleman whose will was probated in Long Island provided that "his negro woman Pegg be given a comfortable support from his residuary estate, and that she be at Liberty to live with such of his Chidren for such times as she shall see fitt."

It sometimes amused slaveowners to educate their slaves. The first black poet in America, Lucy Terry, was a slave in Deerfield, Massachusetts. The piece of verse she produced in 1746 tells the story of an Indian raid on Deerfield with great verve:

> *August 'twas the twenty fifth*
> *Seventeen hundred forty-six*
> *The Indians did in ambush lay*
> *Some very valient men to slay*
> *The names of whom I'll not leave out*
> *Samuel Allen like a hero fout*
> *And though he was so brave and bold*
> *His face no more shall we behold*

Eleazer Hawks was killed outright
Before he had time to fight
Before he did the Indians see
Was shot and killed immediately.
Oliver Amsden he was slain
Which caused his friends much grief and pain.
Samuel Amsden they found dead
Not many rods off from his head.
Adonijah Gillet we do hear
Did lose his life which was so dear.
John Saddler fled across the water
And so excaped the dreadful slaughter
Eunice Allen see the Indians comeing
And hoped to save herself by running
And had not her petticoats stopt her
The awful creatures had not cotched her
And tommyhawked her on the head
And left her on the ground for dead.
Young Samuel Allen, Oh! lack a-day
Was taken and carried to Canada.

Far better known than Lucy Terry is Phillis Wheatley. She was the pampered house slave of Mr. and Mrs. John Wheatley of Boston. She had been purchased directly off an African slave ship in 1761 to serve, it seems, as a household pet. She was a thin, asthmatic child, just losing her front teeth, and must have made a pathetic sight when sold on the auction block. The Wheatley family included teenage twins, Mary and

Nathaniel, who gave a great deal of attention to little Phillis. They delighted in teaching her English. She was naturally bright and had the child's natural ability to learn language quickly. Within sixteen months she not only spoke English but could read even "the most difficult Parts" of the Bible. Pleased by this progress, Mary Wheatley introduced Phillis to Latin. At the age of twelve the black girl was translating Ovid. She was also studying English literature and was particularly attracted by the neoclassical couplets of Alexander Pope. At the age of fourteen she had begun to write poetry of her own.

Phillis was treated by the Wheatley family as an indulged youngest child. She had a room of her own in the house, she dined at the table with the rest of the family, and she did no more work in the house than any well-to-do young woman would do in her own home. By the time she was seventeen she was a member of the Old South Meeting House and had published a poem commemorating the death of the famous minister George Whitefield. Had she been a white woman her precosity and literary productions would have made her remarkable. But as she was a black woman they made her a freak. A Frenchman living in America described her as "one of the strangest creatures in the country and perhaps in the whole world." Mrs. Wheatley encouraged Phillis to accept invitations to visit other upper-class households so that they could examine her in person and marvel at the unexpected spectacle of an educated black. At the age of twenty she was sent to England where she also attracted a great deal of attention and where a full volume of her poetry was published. Yet she must always be aware of her "place," and her place was an awkward one. The Wheatleys could not make her white, but they had made her different from other blacks.

Phillis Wheatley's earliest biographer recorded an incident involving Phillis and another Wheatley servant, the coachman Prince. Prince had been sent to drive Phillis home from one of her visits to a home of "wealth and distinction." The two arrived back home with Phillis seated up front next to Prince. Mrs. Wheatley was very angry. "Do but look at the saucy varlet," she said, "if he hasn't the impudence to sit upon the same seat as my Phillis." Presumably on future trips Phillis sat by herself in the back of the carriage. Yet if she was too good to sit next to a coachman, she was not good enough to sit with white persons of "wealth and distinction." She might dine at home with the Wheatleys but when she was invited out she learned to refuse "the seat offered her at their board, and, requesting that a side-table might be laid for her, dined modestly apart from the rest of the company." How lonely she must have been! The only friend she ever had to whom she could relate on an equal basis was Odour Tanner, a black girl who may have come to America on the same slave ship with Phillis

Wheatley and seems to have been raised as a house pet much as Phillis was.

In 1771 Mary Wheatley married. In 1774 Mrs. Wheatley died. In wartime Boston Phillis Wheatley was left alone. She had been given her freedom but that was not enough to give her happiness. The public lost interest in the spectacle of a black woman writing poetry. She did publish a poem honoring George Washington in April, 1776, and the general invited her to visit with him for half an hour in his camp at Cambridge. Yet she could not support herself writing poetry. In April, 1778, Phillis Wheatley married a free black man named John Peters. He "kept a shop, wore a wig, carried a cane, and felt himself superior to all kinds of labor." He soon deserted her, and Phillis became a domestic in a boarding house. In 1784 she published three more poems. The last of these, entitled "Liberty and Peace," is considered by many to be her best work. Before it was printed, however, Phillis Wheatley was dead. She died in extreme poverty at the age of thirty-one with no company but her infant child. Two children born earlier were already dead, and the baby survived its mother by only a few hours.

The principles of the American Revolution — freedom, equality, and self-determination — had special meaning for black women. Some lines of Phillis Wheatley's poetry reflect what must have been a common emotion even among wholly uneducated slaves:

I, young in life, by seeming cruel fate
Was snatch'd from Afric's fancy'd happy seat;
What pangs excruciating must molest,
What sorrows labour in my parent's breast?
Steel'd was that soul and by no misery mov'd
That from a father seiz'd his babe beloved:
Such, such my case. And can I then but pray
Others may never feel tyrannic sway?

For the black population, the coming of the American
Revolution represented an opportunity for them to gain
their freedom. Both the British and the Americans
offered freedom to blacks who would join the army.
When Lord Dunmore issued his proclamation encouraging both black slaves and white servants to leave their
masters and join the British army, a black woman in New
York City was said to have named her newborn baby in
his honor. Although most of the slaves who responded to
this call were men, some women also went to the British
lines. In December of 1776 nine slaves embarked in an
open boat trying to reach the British base at Norfolk,
Virginia. They were captured and two of the nine were
found to be women. In Philadelphia the British organized a "Company of Black Pioneers," which had such
tasks assigned as "to attend the Scavengers, — assist in
Cleaning the Streets and Removing all Newsiances being
thrown into the Streets." The company consisted of
seventy-two men, fifteen women, and eight children.
Even such lowly service was thought to earn freedom for

the blacks who voluntarily joined the British. A black laundress presented this petition in support of her claim to freedom after the war: "*Please your Excellency* I came from Virginia with General Ashley When I came from there I was quite Naked. I was in Service a year and a half with Mr Savage the remaining Part I was with Lord Dunmore. Washing and ironing in his Service I came with him from Charlestown to New York and was in Service with him till he went away My master came for me I told him I would not go with him One Mr. Yelback wanted to steal me back to Virginia and was not my Master he took all my Cloaths which his Majesty gave me, he said he would hang Major Williams for giving me a Pass he took my Money from me and stole my Child from me and Sent it to Virginia." Hundreds of black women left America with the British troops after the Revolution and went to Canada or the Caribbean islands. Many of these were resold as slaves, but others gained the freedom they had been promised.

Other black women, free as well as slave, supported the Patriot side in the war. A Philadelphia newspaper reported the action of a black woman who spent two dollars she had earned as a laundress to buy the ingredients to make bread and soup for Americans held prisoner by the British. Other black women joined the American army either as servants or as wives of black men who had enlisted on the Patriot side. It was not difficult for slaves to see that the rhetoric of the

Declaration of Independence had relevance to their condition. Indeed, the Revolution encouraged the development of the first abolitionist societies in America and slavery was abolished in the northern states soon after the war. A black slave woman in Massachusetts, Elizabeth Freeman, who was better known as Mumbet, became well-known in 1781 when she successfully sued for her freedom citing the Massachusetts bill of rights.

Mumbet and her sister were slaves of Colonel Ashley of Sheffield, Massachusetts. Her husband had enlisted as a soldier in the Patriot army hoping to win his freedom, but he was killed in battle. One day an argument broke out in the kitchen of the Ashley house. Mrs. Ashley picked up a hot kitchen shovel and swung at Mumbet's sister. Mumbet tried to protect her and took the blow on her arm. The hot shovel left a permanent scar. Mumbet decided she did not have to submit to such treatment and left the Ashley home. She had heard a great deal of discussion about the bill of rights and the new constitution of Massachusetts. "By keepin' still and mindin' things" she had discovered that the law said that all people were born free and equal. She went to a lawyer named Theodore Sedgwick who took her case. The jury agreed with Mumbet's interpretation of the state bill of rights and set her free in August, 1781. Mumbet then became a paid domestic in the Sedgwick home and won the affection and respect of her employers. After her death Theodore Sedgwick paid her this tribute: "If there could be a practical refutation of the imagined superiority of our race to hers, the life and character of this woman would afford that refutation . . . she had nothing of the submissive or subdued character, which succumbs to superior force . . . Even in her humble station, she had, when occasion required it, an air of command which conferred a degree of dignity . . . She claimed no distinction; but it was yielded to her from her superior experience, energy, skills, and sagacity . . . This woman, by her extreme industry and economy, supported a large family . . . She could neither read nor write; yet her conversation was instructive, and her society was much sought after." As she grew older, Mumbet and her daughter moved into a house of their own. Mumbet lived to the age of eighty-five. When she was almost seventy a watercolor portrait was made of her on ivory by a young woman in the Sedgwick family. She is one of a very small number of eighteenth-century black women for whom such a pictoral record exists. Most black women attracted little attention from the white community and so their lives left only slight traces for historians to follow. And despite the success of the abolitionist movement in the northern states, most black women of the eighteenth century lived and died as slaves.

5

NATIVE AMERICAN WOMEN

Gᴇɴᴇʀᴀʟɪᴢᴀᴛɪᴏɴs about the lives of American Indians must always be made with caution. As early as 1633, a French missionary at Quebec pointed out the danger. It had become customary, he said, "after seeing two or three Savages do the same thing, it is at once reported to be a custom of the whole Tribe . . . There are many tribes in these countries who agree in a number of things and differ in many others; so that, when it is said that certain practices are common to the Savages, it may be true of one tribe and not true of another." At the time of the American Revolution, the physical characteristics and the life styles of the native American population differed more widely than the physical characteristics and life styles of Europeans of various nationalities. In North Dakota the Mandan Indians had fair skin, platinum blond hair, and gray eyes at the time of their first contact with white traders. In other areas Indians with coal black hair and black eyes deepened their naturally bronze skin with cosmetic dyes. The eastern Indians apparently had lighter skin, less prominent cheekbones, and generally resembled Europeans more than the Plains Indians did. Yet by the time of the Revolution their practice of freely intermarrying with members of all races — Indian, black, and European — had undoubtedly contributed to their appearance. Life styles of the native Americans differed just as greatly as their appearance. West of the Mississippi, the Indians lived a nomadic life, constantly on the move within the boundaries of vast territories that the tribes loosely identified as their own. They did not yet have horses — these useful animals were introduced to them by Europeans and greatly changed their way of life. In the late eighteenth century their only beasts of burden were dogs. On the other hand, the eastern tribes, particularly the Iroquois in the Northeast and the Five Civilized Tribes of the Southeast, were nearly sedentary. They moved their villages between fixed locations at regular intervals.

It is arbitrary to consider Indian history only for those times and those regions where the Indians and Europeans interacted. Yet it is necessary to restrict the subject in order to generalize. This chapter, then, deals with the native Americans living east of the Mississippi at the time of the Revolution. There were, perhaps, 150,000 of them at a time when the white population was about 1,750,000 and the black population about 500,000. They were mostly members of three different cultural groups. The Iroquois were concentrated in upper New York and included the Mohawk, Oneida, Tuscarora, Onondaga, Cayuga, and Seneca. Also in the Northeast were various tribes identified as Algonquin because they all spoke similar languages. These include the Shawnee, Delaware, Chippewa, Wyandot, Potawatomi, Miami, Ottawa, Winnebago, Monominee, Sauk, and Fox. The Five Civilized Tribes of the Southeast were the Cherokee, Creek, Choctaw, Chickawaw, and Seminole.

By the time of the American Revolution the cultures of all these peoples had undergone great changes. The arrival of vast numbers of Europeans and Africans had introduced new elements into the American environment. Some of these were deadly — foreign diseases, for example — others were welcomed by the Indians as improvements in their lives. Before the arrival of Europeans, the native Americans had been in the Stone Age. That is, they had no metal tools of any kind and made do with implements of stone and bone. These conditions required both men and women in Indian cultures to perfect a wider variety of skills and work harder just to stay alive than was necessary for Europeans. Hard as colonial Americans worked on the early frontier, the native Americans had had to work harder. When they had the opportunity to acquire European goods, the Indians rapidly adapted them to their way of life. By the time of the American Revolution they were no longer Stone Age people and their life styles were considerably different from what they had been a century and a half earlier.

By the middle of the eighteenth century, the way of life of the eastern Indians was wholly dependent on their European neighbors. When they could trade furs for the superior knives, kettles, and needles of the Europeans, there was no reason to continue to practice the arts of pottery-making and fashioning tools out of stone and bones. Yet when these arts had been neglected for a generation, when the oldest Indian to understand them died without passing them on to a younger worker, they could never again be recovered. Although the native Americans increasingly resented the movement of large numbers of foreigners into their lands, their relationship with the colonists was ambivalent. They did not want them moving farther inland, but they could not do without them.

The roles of men and women in the Indian societies had been established under Stone Age conditions. The introduction of European technology made life easier for both sexes, but the general division of labor remained the same. Even the European way of life, after all, required mastery of a substantial number of specialized skills. It was not possible in any preindustrial society to delay training a child for the work it would do later in life for very long after its birth. The tasks to be learned were too many and too complex. Consequently, since it was observed that adult males generally were physically stronger than women, and since it was impossible to delay training a child while it grew to an age where those individual boys and girls who reversed the usual pattern could be identified, all boys were automatically trained to men's work and all girls were trained to do women's work. These roles were not, however, rigidly fixed. Women whose aptitude was clearly directed toward the male role occasionally appear as warriors and even war chiefs without being considered "unnatural" or losing their status as wives and mothers.

In the primitive Indian societies, men's work was hunting and war. This work required muscular exertion, skill in the use of weapons, ability to endure physical hardship, and courage — even foolhardy courage — in the face of danger. Stalking a quick-footed animal until it was in range of a bow and arrow was an art not easily mastered. Much of the Indian hunting was done with traps or by driving the animals into an ambush. Even here, however, there could be danger in a confrontation with a wounded animal. To do his job of providing meat for the tribe, an Indian man had to work constantly to keep himself in top physical condition.

The Indians did not hunt every day of the year. In order to preserve their skills and keep themselves in shape Indian men spent the nonhunting seasons in quasiceremonial raids on Indian enemies or in what the white population sneered at as "games." These games included contests in archery and hatchet throwing, running, and swimming. Only one team sport has been identified: a form of football played on a smooth beach with the goal posts placed a mile apart. Granted that the Indian men may have enjoyed these workouts, which continued for days at a time, they were certainly not idling away their time. Had the men neglected such exercises and chosen instead to sit before their wigwams cooking or sewing as the women did, there would have been precious few deer caught in the next hunting season.

Since hunting, or keeping in shape for hunting, absorbed all of the Indian man's time, all the other work of the tribe was done by the women. She raised all the food crops, cooked, sewed, built the wigwams, and even dragged home the carcasses after a successful hunt. The Europeans pitied her as a drudge. Since there was always danger when walking through the woods and only the man was trained in the use of weapons, a company of Indians always moved through the forest "Indian file." The men went first, so they would make first contact with any enemy. They carried nothing but their weapons so that these would be ready for instant use. The women followed behind carrying burdens of great weight, presenting a contrast with their unburdened husbands that shocked the Europeans. "Their women were their mules," exclaimed an early French explorer. The status of Indian women was not, however, as depressed as it appeared to the casual observer. Indian men held women's work in high regard. They were well aware that the skills of the women and their ability to carry heavy loads were indispensable to Indian living and normally impossible for men to duplicate. It took the European men some time to realize that the Indians were right when they declared that it was absolutely necessary for them to take women along on expeditions into the interior. Male guides would not be adequate. As one Indian man explained, "Women were made for labor; one of them can carry, or haul, as much as two men can do. They pitch our tents, make and mend our clothing, keep us warm at night; and, in fact, there is no such thing as travelling any considerable distance, or for any length of time, in this country, without their assistance." After a few disastrous experiences, the Europeans learned to include wives as well as husbands when they hired Indian guides.

The histories of exploration pass over the Indian women, ignoring their roles as guides, interpreters, and diplomats during expeditions into the interior as well as their hard work. But they were there. Alexander Mackenzie's expedition to the Arctic Ocean in 1789 included two women who were brought along to make

moccasins. A woman managed one of his canoes. Early
explorations in the Southwest and the Rockies included
women who sewed, cooked, and carried. The only
Indian guide woman who has attracted any attention is
Sacajawea, who accompanied the Lewis and Clark expedition. Contrary to the popular legend, Sacajawea did
not show Lewis and Clark the way to the Pacific.
Although she was a valuable member of the expedition,
her functions were the traditional ones. She was an
interpreter, she gathered food and cooked, and on one
occasion she saved some valuable records and scientific
apparatus from being washed overboard. Captain Clark
obviously admired her and after her death in 1812 at the
age of twenty-five, he adopted and raised her two
children.

Sacajawea was a member of the Shoshoni tribe, which
inhabited what is now central Idaho. Her proficiency in
trail skills was well developed because her people were
nomadic and spent most of their time traveling. Eastern
Indian women, however, traveled much less. Their skills
were primarily agricultural. The importance of this
activity was so great that women's work was respected
even more among eastern Indians than it was among
those who found most of their food supply by simple
hunting and foraging. Meriwether Lewis pointed out
that "the importance of the female in savage life, has no
necessary relation to the virtues of the men, but is
regulated wholly by their capacity to be useful . . .

Where the women can aid in procuring subsistence for the tribe, they are treated with more equality, and their importance is proportioned to the share which they take in that labor; while in countries where subsistence is chiefly procured by the exertions of the men, the women are considered and treated as burdens." Among eastern Indians the labor of the women provided most of the tribal diet.

The eastern Indian diet was based primarily on vegetables. The native Americans consumed less meat per capita than either the colonists or their black slaves and substantially less than modern Americans. The Europeans tended to overestimate the degree to which the native Americans depended on hunting for their food. Actually, the crops cultivated by the women were basic except in the northern part of Maine, where the growing season was short. Corn was the staple crop. Beans, squash, and pumpkins were also cultivated. Patriot soldiers who penetrated into Iroquois country in 1779 were amazed at the extensive acreage the Indian women had under cultivation. All of the agricultural work was theirs except for the original clearing of the land. Planting, cultivating, and harvesting were all women's work — and most of it was done with wooden spades and stone hoes until metal tools were brought in by the Europeans.

Not only were women responsible for the cultivation of basic crops, but they added to the food supply in other

ways as well. In the summer and autumn, wild fruits and
berries were gathered. Cranberries were especially valued. When dried for the winter, these provided the only
source of vitamin C available to the Indians. In the
summer, if the tribe was accustomed to make a camp by
the ocean, the women foraged for lobsters, crabs, clams
and other shellfish. Some of this food, too, was dried for
winter use. The meat provided by the hunters was rarely
preserved. The Indians had neither salt nor vinegar for
preserving. Smoking and drying were the only preserva-
tive methods they used. While meat could be dried, and
sometimes was for use by war parties, the Indians
preferred their meat fresh. So long as the hunters were
healthy and the game was plentiful, the tribe could enjoy
venison, bear, beaver, and moose meat, as well as turkey,
duck, or pigeon along with its corn puddings.

The absence of salt in the recipes and the assumption
that Indians regularly ate the sort of food that their war
parties carried as emergency rations, gave the Europeans
a poor opinion of Indian cuisine. Men traveling without
women were obliged to eat what they could carry with
them or what they could fix for themselves. Colonists
captured by Indians reported being fed such items as
undercooked moose meat, horse, dog, and beaver guts.
The basic trail ration was prepared by the Indian women.
It was so vital to the success of a war party that the
women could effectively veto a declaration of war by
refusing to supply it. The trail ration could be prepared

according to a variety of recipes. It might be as simple as corn meal mixed with maple sugar or as complex as the pemmican prepared by Indians in the northern prairie states. Pemmican was made from dried buffalo meat, pounded into a powder by placing it between two hides and beating it with stones. This was then mixed with melted buffalo fat and dried cranberries. Pemmican was traditionally carried in ninety pound bags. It would keep for years and provided a great deal of nourishment and calories relative to its weight. It was said that "even the gluttonous french canadian that devours eight pounds of fresh meat every day is contented with one and a half pounds per day."

Pemmican was an emergency ration. In preparing everyday meals for their families, Indian women might prepare a variety of relatively sophisticated dishes. The most common dish was basically a corn meal pudding to which other food was added. Bits of meat or beans might be boiled with the corn together with a selection of seasonings. Although they did not use salt, Indian women flavored their food with pounded hazelnuts, dried pumpkin blossoms, trout herb, wild ginger, bearberry, mountain mint, and maple sugar. The meal might also include broiled meat of some sort, birds' eggs, and a selection of nuts and berries. They commonly ate from individual wooden bowls using their fingers. Their beverage was water. They did not generally keep cows for their milk, and they knew nothing of brewing alcoholic beverages. When they learned of alcohol from the Europeans a few tribes began to make their own cider and rum. Most, however, recognizing the dangers of alcoholism, regarded it as a poison.

Although the Indians welcomed European cooking utensils and such new food items as pork, it was the Europeans who learned about food from the Indians. Many of the foods indigenous to North America were unfamiliar to Europeans and they learned how to prepare them from the Indians. New England women prepared American kidney beans and lima beans in earthenware crocks buried in pits filled with hot ashes and stones. They also copied the Indian "clam-bake" recipe. The basic ingredients were clams, corn, and seaweed, but other shellfish might be added too. The cook dug a pit and lined it with flat stones. These were heated by building a hot fire on them. When they were white hot, the burning embers were brushed off and a layer of seaweed was placed on top of the stones. Then alternate layers of clams, ears of corn, and additional seaweed were piled up until the pit was full. Then a damp hide was laid over the pit and kept moist while the meal was cooking. An hour or so later, the pit was opened and there was a feast of clams and corn that was moist, tender, and delicious. Just as the best in Southern cooking seems to have come from the black women's influence, the native American women seem to have given us much of the best in New England cuisine.

Cooking was a feature of women's work that was familiar to European women. The Indian conception of woman as "homemaker" was something else again. The Indian women literally made the family home; she built it and she carried it from place to place on her back when the tribe moved to new quarters. Little girls were trained to carry bundles of wood for the fire that were made heavier and heavier as they grew older until they could carry a whole night's supply in one trip. At the same time they were taught to make miniature huts or wigwams for their dolls in order to master the technique. A mother would say to her daughter, "You must not grow up to live outdoors and be made fun of because you do not know how to make a good wigwam." By the time of the Revolution some tribes had forgotten the skills involved in building homes and lived in log cabins just as the Europeans did. But most found their old dwellings more comfortable and did not attempt to imitate the homes of colonial women.

One great advantage of the Indian dwellings was their portability. Even the most sedentary tribes shifted their dwellings with some regularity. Indians might move their homes for a variety of reasons. If a family member died, if there was sickness in the neighborhood, or if lice and fleas became a nuisance, moving was a sensible procedure. Among highly nomadic tribes a home site was abandoned permanently. They left nothing behind and after a year had passed grass grew over the tepee floors and only the mixture of some untended beans and corn in the natural grasses revealed that the area had once been a town. More settled Indians moved between fixed homesites and often left the frames of their houses in place when they made a seasonal move. It was customary to have a spring home near the fields where the women planted their crops, a summer home by the ocean where the men would fish and the women gather shellfish, and a winter home in a sheltered valley protected from the cold winds.

All Indians did not build the same kind of home. The largest structures were the longhouses built by the Iroquois. An Iroquois town might cover ten acres, and one house might be as long as three hundred feet. A number of families who were related to each other shared a house. They built it long enough so that no group of relatives would be left out. The house was built by forcing rows of forked poles into the ground four or five feet apart. Cross poles were placed on top to form an arched roof. These were strengthened by an arrangement of rafters and transverse poles all tied together securely. The women then added large sheets of bark to the frames, which were held in place, rough side out, by another series of poles. Holes were left in the roof at intervals of about twenty feet. These were covered with loose pieces of bark so they could be opened and closed by using a pole inside the house. A stone hearth was built on the ground under each hole. The door at each end of the house was either hide or bark. Often a storage porch was built at the ends of the house so that no family would sleep near the drafty entrance.

Inside, these homes were snug but smoky. The Indians did not share the European desire for privacy and appreciated the greater warmth of a home where many people lived in close quarters. The inside of an Iroquois longhouse or an Algonquin wigwam contained no furniture, although some Indians had low platforms built around the walls that served as chairs, shelves, and beds. The roof poles were used to hang weapons, clothes, hemp bags containing food, and other possessions. Some tribes covered the inside walls with embroidered mats, which insulated the home and added a touch of color.

Although colonial women might not have appreciated their Indian sisters' building skills, they did appreciate their talent as needle artists. Indian women were expert at many kinds of handwork. Men made their own weapons and canoes, but women manufactured almost everything else. They spun hemp with stone spindles rolled against their thighs and wove it into fishnets. They made the bark panels for the sides of the longhouse or wove mats of rushes for the wigwam. They made baskets, bowls, and agricultural tools. And, of course, they made clothing. Unlike the colonists, however, who needed clothing for warmth and to protect their modesty, the Indians wore clothing primarily as decoration.

The native Americans were not disturbed by nudity.

Like the Africans, they lacked the concept of sex as dirty or sinful, and they were more sensitive than the Europeans to matters of personal cleanliness. Both men and women bathed frequently, which the Europeans regarded as one sign of their savagery. The agents of Queen Isabella who were charged with the mission of civilizing the Indians in 1503 were told "They are not to bathe as frequently as hitherto." Because clothing was difficult to keep clean, they normally wore very little. Except on ceremonial occasions or in extremely cold weather, men wore only a loincloth and moccasins and women moccasins and a knee-length skirt. They protected themselves from the summer sun, the winter chill, mosquitoes and fleas by coating themselves with vegetable or animal fats. A variety of substances was used for this purpose, and some of them, no doubt, smelled rather odd. Yet they probably smelled no worse than the average colonist. And, as an Indian woman explained to a colonist who asked why she refused to wear English clothes, the natives "had rather goe naked than be lousie." Since their tightly made, crowded, windowless homes were considerably warmer than those of the colonists, the Indians remained quite comfortable in a layer of bear grease or fish oil while their European neighbors shivered in layers of shawls and quilted petticoats.

Clothing serves an important function in addition to providing warmth and concealing sex differences. Psychologists recognize that we use our clothing to project our feelings about ourselves. The Indians dressed up to show they felt splendid. Indeed, despite their customary nudity, the Indians displayed so much personal ornamentation as to appear gaudy. Women painted their faces even for everyday and men used paint for special ceremonies. Both sexes were fond of jewelry. They wore earrings, bracelets, necklaces, belts, and copper breastplates even without other clothing. When they "dressed up," the garments themselves were viewed merely as a base on which to lay further decoration. Indian embroidery patterns included ceremonial symbols, purely decorative forms, and certain conventional symbols that could be used in series to tell a story. Indians who were proud of certain events in their lives might have the entire episode embroidered on to the costumes they wore for special celebrations. The women who made such garments for themselves and members of their family were the artists and the historians of their people. In particular, the beadwork "wampum belts" that were given to confirm bargains or treaties were treasured by the tribe and served as the only form of national record.

Although Indian women were skilled in a wide variety of embroidery techniques, including some forms employing feathers, fish skin, and appliqué in furs, the oldest and most universally practiced were porcupine-quill embroidery and beadwork. One of the earliest travelers to America wrote, "The women manifest much ingenuity and taste in the work which they execute with porcupine quills. The color of these quills is various, beautiful and desirable, and the art of dyeing them is practiced only by the females." As in European embroidery, dyeing was an essential part of the art. Indian women discovered the coloring properties of a variety of barks, berries, flowers, and some mineral materials. When they obtained European cloth, they boiled it to release its dye and so added some new colors to their store. The dyed quills were kept in sacks made of animal gut so the various shades would be available as they were needed to work a particular pattern. The embroidery was worked on deerskin that had been carefully tanned and softened until it was as soft and smooth as woven cloth. White buckskin was especially beautiful. The quills were fastened to the skin with a thin strip of sinew. They were doubled back and forth to hide the stitches. The stitches did not penetrate the hide, but ran only through the upper surface. Thus, when the work was completed no stitches showed on top and the back surface was perfectly smooth.

Indian beadwork often used the same designs as quill embroidery. The Indians had beads of their own made from minerals, seeds, and animal horns, teeth or claws, as well as from shells. The smooth, vividly colored glass beads brought to America by the Europeans, however, were far superior. It was the dedication of the Indians to their women's embroidery art that explains the high regard the natives had for traders' beads. Beads were strung on short sinew threads and sewn together in rows to fill in a design area. Native beads or animal teeth or even pearls might be mixed with the glass beads in order to achieve a special effect. The glowing color of this embroidery on a base of soft deerskin produced a spectacle of extraordinary beauty especially when it was viewed on the bodies of dancers in the light of a council fire.

Despite a division of labor along sex lines that convinced Europeans that the lot of Indian women was the lowest form of servitude, they actually enjoyed greater economic, social, and political status than colonial women did. Because of the Indians' casual attitude toward sex and willingness to practice abortion there was no double standard. A surprised European noted that among the Hurons "a young woman is allowed to do what she pleases; let her conduct be what it will, neither father nor mother, brother nor sister, can pretende to control her. A young woman, say they, is master of her own body, and by her natural right to liberty is free to do what she pleases." Native Americans were astonished by what seemed to them the European male's preoccupation with sex. To them it was merely an ordinary part of life. They did not find themselves in situations that encouraged rape or other crimes of "passion." Marriage, to them, was a personal matter between two individuals. It had neither legal nor religious significance. They had no concept of a baby being "illegitimate." Divorce was as easy for a woman as for a man. Indeed, the common form was for the woman to pile her husband's belongings outside the door to indicate that he was no longer part of the family. Divorce was uncommon once a couple had children, but childless couples felt no compulsion to stay together any longer than it pleased them to do so. A party of colonial army officers watched in astonishment as the women in an eighteenth-century Shawnee village held a mass divorce party. It consisted of a three-day celebration during which the women sang, "I am not afraid of my husband, I will choose what man I please." Then the men of the village danced past the women, each chose the man she wanted and took him home with her. Such communal "orgies" did not prevent the Indians from having strong family relationships.

Often what the Europeans viewed as sexual orgies were religious fertility rites. Many tribes apparently venerated their women for their fertility. There were certain magic rituals which only women could perform. Although the "medicine men" or "powwows" who communicated with the spirit world through dreams were usually men, women might also be recognized in such roles. The Indian nations generally recognized the mothers as the center of their community. Descent was traced through the mothers. The chief or sachem was usually a man who inherited his position from his mother's family. However, a woman, too, might become a sachem if she demonstrated the necessary qualities of leadership. The mothers of the tribe had their own council and their opinions were respected. They might have final say on a question when the warrior's council disagreed, and they could prevent their tribe from going to war by refusing to provide trail rations and moccasins. Under Indian custom the mothers also had the final decision as to the fate of captives taken during war.

The function of war in Indian society was chiefly ritualistic. Until the European's made war a question of their survival as a people, the Indians warred with each other partly for the sport, partly to take captives for adoption into the tribe, and partly to have victims for religious practices that demanded human sacrifice. The mothers of the tribe decided whether an individual captive should be adopted or put to death with ghastly tortures. These gruesome religious practices are certainly the least attractive feature of Indian life. In fairness, however, it must be recognized that Europeans of that age whipped, castrated, burned alive, disemboweled, and beheaded persons convicted of various crimes. The Indians limited their mayhem to foreigners and made one victim go a long way. Most of the captives taken in war were accepted as members of the tribe and became in all ways equal to those who had been born into it. They appear to have been entirely free of race prejudice. They would adopt Europeans and Africans as well as captives from alien Indian nations.

Perhaps the most convincing judgment to non-Indians

on the merits of Indian life was that passed on it by
European captives. It appears that as many as three
quarters of those white captives adopted into Indian tribes
may have preferred to stay with the Indians. Benjamin
Franklin noted this phenomenon in 1753: "When an
Indian Child has been brought up among us, taught our
language and habituated to our Customs, yet if he goes to
see his relations and makes one Indian Ramble with them,
there is no perswading him ever to return. [But] when
white persons of either sex have been taken prisoners
young by the Indians, and lived a while among them, tho'
ransomed by their Friends, and treated with all imaginable tenderness to prevail them to stay among the English,
yet in a Short time they become disgusted with our
manner of life, and the care and pains that are necessary
to support it, and take the first good Opportunity of
escaping again to the Woods, from whence there is no
reclaiming them." Those Europeans who had no direct
experience of Indian life could not understand how a
white person could embrace it or even why the Indians
did not enthusiastically convert to European civilization.
Writing of those white captives who refused to return
from the woods one such wrote, "For the honour of
humanity we would suppose those persons to have been
of the lowest rank, either bred up in ignorance and
distressing penury, or who had lived so long with the
Indians as to forget all their former connections. For,
easy and unconstrained as the savage life is it could never

be put in competition with the blessings of improved life and the light of religion, by any persons who have had the happiness of enjoying, and the capacity of discerning, them." Most Europeans did not think it should take much discernment for the Indians to realize how much better European life was. A Puritan minister wrote in surprise, "Tho' they saw a People Arrive among them, who were Clothed in *Habits* of much more Comfort and Splendour, than what there was to be seen in the *Rough Skins* with which they hardly covered themselves; and who had Houses full of Good Things, vastly out-shining their squalid and dark *Wigwams;* And they saw this People Replenishing their *Fields,* with *Trees* and with *Grains,* and useful *Animals,* which until now they had been wholly Strangers to; yet they did not seem touch'd in the least, with any *Ambition* to come at such Desireable Circumstances . . ."

Most of those captured for adoption were women or very young children. They were treated with as much respect and affection as the deceased family member whom their adoption was intended to replace. They had complete freedom of movement, were encouraged — but not forced — to marry, and could rise to positions of great prominence. Mary Jemison, who spent a long life with the Indians after being captured at the age of twelve, wrote fondly of her Indian sisters: "I was ever considered and treated by them as a real sister the same as though I had been born of their mother." She did not consider

Indian women's work as hard as that of white women. They had a smaller number of chores to perform, she said, they could work at their own pace without anyone to hurry them along, and they were not bothered with "spinning, weaving, sewing, stocking knitting," and similar endless chores.

There seems to be no question that children were happier raised by the Indians. Observers all agreed that the Indians were very fond of their children and they showed equal affection to those they adopted. The Indians thought the European customs of beating their children, training them in stern Calvinistic morality, requiring them to wear clothing, and discouraging play and demonstrations of affection were cruel and unnatural. The little children seemed to agree and regularly chose their Indian mothers over their natural mothers when given a choice. Many could only be brought back to white society tied hand and foot and then must be watched constantly or they would run away to their Indian families.

The Indians played a central role in the war known as the American Revolution. To them, however, the dispute between the English colonists and the mother country were peripheral. For the Indians the conflict was a war for Indian independence, and whichever side they chose they lost it. Mary Brant was a powerful influence among the Iroquois. She was a Mohawk, the leader of the society of all Iroquois matrons, and the widow of Sir

William Johnson, Superintendent of Indian Affairs. Her brother, Joseph Brant, is the best-known Indian warrior of the Revolution, yet she may have exerted even more influence in the Confederacy than he did. A British Indian agent declared that "one word from her goes farther with them [the Iroquois] than a thousand from any white man without exception." She used her influence to keep the western tribes of Iroquois loyal to George III. When the Americans won the war she and her tribe had to abandon their lands and retreat to Canada. On the other side, Nancy Ward held positions of authority in the Cherokee nation. She had fought as a warrior in a war against the Creeks and in reward of her heroism was made "Beloved Woman" of the tribe. This office made her chief of the women's council and a member of the council of chiefs. She was friendly with the white settlers and supported the Patriots during the Revolution. Yet the Cherokees too lost their land. In 1817, when she was nearly eighty, she sent her last message to the council of chiefs urging them not to surrender any more territory. The pressures were too great, however. Nancy Ward was forced to leave her village of Chota. She opened an inn near what is now Benton, Tennessee and, like Mary Brant, died away from her home. For the native Americans, the War for American Independence was a war they could not win.

6

LOYALIST WOMEN

THERE were relatively few newspapers in eighteenth-century America. Most people had little contact with events outside their own neighborhoods. Except in urban areas and along the Atlantic coast, few Americans became deeply aroused over matters like the Stamp Act and the tea tax. They did not care about politics. They only wanted to be left alone. Once the war began, however, armies, militia units, and local committees of safety appeared in the countryside. People in all parts of the country found that they could no longer ignore politics. The movements of armies politicized the population, and all those who refused to join the Patriots were classified as Loyalists.

People decided which side to support for very personal reasons. Even members of the same family might react to events differently. Suppose, for example, that a party of Loyalist militia tramped mud into the house, stole the chickens in the yard, and threatened to tar and feather anyone who would not swear allegiance to King George. Some members of the family might be glad enough to swear just to get the men out of the house. Others might grow angry enough to join a local Patriot organization for revenge. When partisans of both sides operated in the same area, as they often did, some individuals might be Loyalists one day and Patriots the next, whichever seemed safer.

Men soon found that they could not safely remain neutral or become known as trimmers. The dedicated Americans on both sides considered a neutral to be a traitor. Women, however, could remain neutral more easily than men. Since they had no property that could be confiscated and were not expected to have political opinions, they might be able to escape making a commitment to either side. Although it did not always work, many women were able to use their sex as a reason for not taking sides. Grace Growden Galloway, whose husband was an exiled Loyalist, managed to avoid exile herself. "As I never Meddle with politics," she wrote, "I hope never to give any Just Reason of Offence." Again she wrote, "I am determin'd not to write anything that can endanger either Church or state & as a Woman I

cannot or at least I will not be a Traytor to either side."
She had her own views, however, and thought that as a
woman (whose ideas must be inconsequential) she ought
to be allowed to write without censorship. "I wish the
Nobel [sic] Minded Hero's on both sides wou'd let Us
women write without inspecting our scrawls," she wrote
to her daugher, "for I find the restraint both disagreeable
and Mortifying."

Since, as a practical matter, it was harder for women
than for men to resist an armed force, women forced to
choose sides often chose whichever appeared stronger.
Thus when the British occupied the City of Philadelphia,
the young women who cared more for their social lives
than for politics were glad to accept invitations to the
officers' balls. The Patriot governor of New Jersey
angrily wrote, "the Philadelphia flirts are equally famous
for their want of modesty and want of patriotism in their
over complaisance to red-coats . . . who could not
conquer the men of the country but everywhere they
have taken the women almost without a trial — damn
them." In fairness it should be recognized that the British
took many women against their will. On their march
toward Philadelphia through New Jersey it was reported
that "they to the disgrace of a civilis'd nation ravish the
fair sex from the age of ten to seventy." And as another
man reported, "They play the very devil with the girls
and even old women to satisfy their libidinous appetites.

There is scarce a virgin to be found in the part of the
country they have pass'd thro'."

Loyalist women from areas occupied by Patriots often
fled to the occupied cities for safety. It would not be
surprising to find that the women in such cities were
largely Loyalist. The experiences of such urban women,
however, often turned them into Patriots. The British
soldiers had difficulty distinguishing between Loyal and
Patriot Americans. Since so many Americans changed
their politics every time the balance of power shifted, it is
understandable that the occupying forces grew confused.
The result, however, was that they often abused Americans who supported the King's cause or who, at least,
were far from being active Patriots. When such people
were insulted or attacked by British soldiers, they
naturally grew to resent the occupying force. Living for
any time in an occupied town seems to have turned many
Loyal women into Patriots.

A Patriot woman who visited her daughter and
son-in-law in New York City during its occupation by
the British reported that their politics were changing.
"The sentiments of a great number have undergone a
thorough change since they have been with the British
army," she noted with satisfaction, "as they have many
opportunities of seeing flagrant acts of injustice and
cruelty of which they could not have believed their
friends capable. This convinces them that if they

conquer, we must live in abject slavery." Her own daughter's political principles had become "perfectly *rebellious,*" and she was hopeful that the whole family would soon be firm Patriots.

Similarly, after Philadelphia was occupied, many women who had earlier feared the war now grew to hate the army. Benjamin Rush reported on his wife's developing Patriotism: "The women of America have at last become principals in the glorious American controversy . . . My dear wife, who you know in the beginning of the war had all the timidity of her sex as to the issue of the war . . . is now so thoroughly enlisted in the cause of her country that she reproaches me with lukewarmness." In occupied Charleston, the women were known to be more rabid Patriots than the men. They took advantage of the British officers' respect for "ladies" to flaunt their political opinions. One officer reported that "The men being prisoners do not dare to speak out, but the women make full amends for their silence, they amuse themselves by teaching their children the principles of rebellion, and seem to take care that the rising generation should be as troublesome as themselves."

In the countryside, where women were left at home to manage the farm and hold off parties of militia demanding food, husbands and sons were not released for military service gladly. Flirtatious American girls often went out to watch the troops march by, and their attentions encouraged desertions on both sides. Many a Hessian soldier took a Pennsylvania Dutch wife and traded his bayonet for a plow. On the other hand, Washington had to deal with the problems created when wives wrote to their husbands in the Continental army begging them to return home before the farm failed and the children starved. One wife wrote, "I am without bread and cannot get any, the Committee [of Safety] will not supply me, my children will starve or if they do not, they must freeze, we have no wood, neither can we get any — Pray come home!" During the winter at Valley Forge Washington gave orders not to allow any unfamiliar women into the camp because so many wives had come to entice their men to return home.

Women had reasons of their own for supporting the Loyalist or the Patriot cause. They did not placidly follow the political views of their male relatives. A large number of families were torn apart. "Everywhere distrust, fear, hatred, and abominable selfishness were met with," wrote the Reverend Nicholas Collin. "Parents and children, brothers and sisters, wife and husband, were enemies to one another." Examples of husbands and wives who chose opposite sides are plentiful. A New Jersey Whig sought to prevent quarrels by painting the words "No Tory talk here" over the mantelpiece as a warning to his Loyalist wife. In South Carolina, the Loyalist Elizabeth Henry and her Whig husband could not keep politics out of their conversations. He finally turned her out of the house. In Pennsylvania, Quaker

Lydia Darrah carried intelligence to the Patriots without the knowledge of her Loyalist husband. She demurely assured the British General Howe that all the family was in bed when his staff had discussed their plans in her home. When later asked how she had justified telling a lie she replied, "Husband and wife are one, and that one is the husband, and my husband was in bed."

Many families were divided when the husband fled to England. It was often charged that husbands and wives who separated in this way during the war did so in a cynical attempt to protect their property. A "Loyalist" husband in England who left his "Patriot" wife in America could hope to return after the war and keep the family estate free from confiscation no matter which side won. It is difficult to tell how often this may have been the case. Certainly it would not work at all unless the wife persuaded her neighbors that her Patriotism was sincere. Commonly the best such a wife could hope for was that the state would consider her husband legally dead. Then she might reclaim her dowry and inherit a widow's share of the family property. The experience of the Chandler family of Worcester, Massachusetts, was fairly typical. John Chandler served with the British army and left the country when the army evacuated Boston. The Massachusetts legislature declared him a permanent exile. Two thirds of his real and personal property were confiscated by the Worcester Committee of Correspondence. Mrs. Chandler was given a lifetime interest in the remaining third so long as she remained in the United States. The couple was never reunited, but the one third of the property Mrs. Chandler retained was eventually passed on to their children. Nothing definite is known of Mrs. Chandler's political views or why she chose not to go to England with her husband. Perhaps saving the property was the important consideration.

There are, however, numerous clear examples of wives who thought their husbands were wicked or stupid when they chose to leave the country. For instance, Samuel Quincy left his wife and family in Massachusetts in May, 1775, despite the protests of his sister. "Let it not be told in America and let it not be told in Great Britain," she wrote him, "that a brother . . . fled from his country — the wife of his youth — the children of his affection — and from his aged sire." For years afterward he tried to persuade his wife, Sophia Quincy, to join him abroad, but she never did. Her political principles at least partly explain her determination to stay in America. Judge Samuel Curwen of Boston and his wife fought bitterly over his decision to leave the country in 1775. Finally she encouraged him to get out of the house meanwhile denouncing him as a runaway. The two never forgave each other. The judge left explicit orders in his will that he not be buried next to his wife since he did not want to awake on the Day of Judgment and find her next to him.

It is likely that a good many marriages that broke up during the Revolution involved husbands and wives who

used the political situation as an excuse to dissolve a union
that was already troubled. An example is the marriage of
Joseph and Grace Growden Galloway. Joseph Galloway
was a leading Loyalist and had collaborated with the
British during their occupation of Philadelphia. When
the British evacuated the city in June, 1778, he knew that
he must leave the city or be punished by the Patriots as a
traitor. But his wife refused to go. Although all of the
family estate was confiscated by the Patriots, she hoped to
claim part of it as her own and save it for her daughter.
She hoped to prevent the execution of the law which
clearly stated that all of a wife's property belongs to her
husband. Although her husband and daughter left without her and she was quickly evicted from her home,
Grace Growden Galloway never rejoined her family.
In her letters to them she complained about the loss of
her property and her misery in being separated from
her loved ones. But her personal diary tells a different
story.

Mrs. Galloway had never resigned herself to the
limitations placed on wives. As a girl she had even
written a bit of verse on the subject although she did not
heed the advice herself:

> *Dear Polly attend the advice of a friend*
> *and never get Tyed to a Man*
> *for when once you are yoked Tw'all a mere Joke*
> *of seeing your freedom again*

After her husband left her, she wrote, "the Liberty of doing as I please Makes even poverty more agreeable than any time I ever spent since I married." She told her diary that she was "easey Nay happy not to be with him & if he is safe I want not to be kept so like a slave as he allways Made Me in preventing every wish of my heart." She grew angry when she learned that the deed to a piece of property she considered her own was recorded only in her husband's name. She blamed him for following what was, after all, the customary legal form. She wrote in her diary, "I would embrace poverty much soon[er] than live with a man who wou'd Grasp at all I have yet treat me worse than a slave." Thanks to the Revolutionary War, Mrs. Galloway found a respectable pretense for living alone.

Of course many separations that occurred during the war reflected no differences — political or otherwise — between the parties. They reflect the attempts of individuals to deal as best they could with a world disrupted by events they did not understand. The case of Susannah and William Marshall provides an example. The Marshalls kept a tavern in Baltimore. Politically, they were neutral. But in 1775 William was forced to choose between joining the American army or being identified as a traitor. He chose to leave the country. For a while Susannah ran the tavern by herself. The Patriots distrusted her, however, and the work must have been hard. Within a few months she sold her property, chartered a schooner to carry what goods she could, and tried to join a British convoy to England. The fleet was gone before she reached the mouth of Chesapeake Bay. She turned around and sailed to another location in Maryland, bought another tavern, and even took over the local ferry service. Here, too, however, she was dissatisfied and in 1777 made another attempt to reach England and rejoin her husband. She chartered another ship and sailed for the West Indies. By a piece of bad luck, two of her crew turned out to be American deserters. A Patriot ship pursued and captured hers. Before the Americans could confiscate their prize, the ship was retaken by a British vessel. Mrs. Marshall did not profit from this reversal, however. The British confiscated all of her ship's cargo and gave her nothing but a passage to England. When she finally reached England she learned that her husband was dead. She tried to support herself and her children by practicing medicine. Finally, the British government granted her a small pension.

After the Revolution, many Americans, like Mrs. Marshall, who had left the country, petitioned the English government for pensions or other relief. These petitions record many pathetic stories involving women whose only crime was neutrality or, at most, choosing the wrong side. Many appear to have been confused victims of events they could not understand. One such was Margaret Frances Hill, housekeeper to the Loyalist

Colonel Guy Johnson. She was, she told the British, "stripped naked of all her Cloaths confined to a cold Room in Bedford New England" for three months during the winter because she had refused a bribe to poison her master. The members of the Loyal Jarvis family, both parents and four children, were rounded up in the middle of the night by the Connecticut Patriots. All of them were stripped naked, loaded on whale boats and abandoned in waist deep water off the shores of Long Island. A most pathetic story is told by Polly Dibblee. She was a member of a prominent Connecticut family and her husband was a lawyer. His political views were unacceptable to the local Patriots and he was forced to flee with his family to Long Island. Five times the family was plundered, stripped of everything they owned, and forced to move from place to place until they finally settled in Canada. Filer Dibblee was now deeply in debt, and spending the long Canadian winter in a rough log cabin further depressed him. Finally, his wife reported, one afternoon "whilst the Famely were at Tea, Mr. Dibblee walked back and forth in the Room, seemingly much composed: but unobserved he took a Razor from the Closet, threw himself on the bed, drew the Curtains, and cut his own Throat." Polly Dibblee tried to carry on, but shortly after her husband's death her cabin burned down. This unfortunate woman rebuilt the cabin only to have it burn again within a year.

There appear to have been substantially fewer politically active women on the British side than on the American. A majority of American women were probably apolitical or at least inactive during the war. Most who did become involved in the conflict appear to have acted only in self-defense. Relatively few Loyalist women believed strongly enough in the British cause to intervene aggressively. In contrast to the many flourishing Daughters of Liberty organizations, organizations of Loyalist women appear to have been virtually nonexistent. In Boston Mrs. Elisha Hutchinson was president of a club consisting of only eight Loyalist women. They met twice a week and were said to "keep up their spirits strangely." It does not appear, however, that they ever did anything more formidable than to drink tea with great ostentation. Meanwhile the local Daughters of Liberty kept an eye on them by appointing a committee "to examine the Tory ladies." In New York an organization of Loyalist women was somewhat more effective. The women were able to raise enough money to purchase a ship and outfit it as a privateer to operate against the Patriots. The vessel was christened appropriately "The Fair American." Although Loyalist records in general are very full, few other references to organizations of Loyalist women exist — a sharp contrast to the extensive activity of Daughters of Liberty groups. Thus the Loyalist women share in what was a weakness of the Loyalist movement itself: a failure of organization.

As individuals, however, Loyalist women were cer-

tainly capable of ingenuity and heroism equal to that of
Patriot women. In Boston Margaret Draper, whose
family had been provincial printers for Massachusetts for
three generations, insisted on keeping the *Massachusetts
Gazette and Boston Weekly Newsletter* Loyal. When her
husband died, she broke with his partner who was a
Patriot and ran the paper herself during the British
occupation. In Charleston, Louisa Wells continued to
run her father's newspaper after he went to England. She
married a Mr. Aikman, one of her father's apprentices.
The paper remained Loyal until she followed her father
into exile. Another woman who tried to use the power of
the press to attack the Patriot cause was Mrs. Charles
Slocum of Rhode Island. She was pilloried, branded on
both cheeks, and had her ears cut off when she was
discovered passing counterfeit Continental currency.

Many Loyalist women claimed that they should be
immune from harsh treatment because of their sex. The
Patriots apparently felt that women who actively participated in the war forfeited claims to special treatment. For
instance, Lorenda Holmes of New York was actively
engaged as a courier for the British. She repeatedly
carried letters through the British lines. Eventually the
Patriots captured her. They were delighted to "have got
the Damned Tory the penny Post at last." They
stripped her naked and searched her for letters, but she
herself admitted that she was not otherwise injured. Her
Loyalist activities continued after this first discovery. In

addition to carrying letters, she began to aid Loyalists who wished to join the British army to get past the Patriot lines. When she was captured a second time, the Patriots were less gentle. She was told to remove her shoes. A soldier then took "a shovel of Wood Coals from the fire and by mere force held Your Memorialists right foot upon the Coals until he had burnt it in a most shocking manner and left Your Memorialist saying that he would learn her to carry off Loyalists to the British Army." This treatment was effective: Lorenda Holmes left the country.

A good many Loyalist women, in addition to Lorenda Holmes, became spies or couriers for the British. Elizabeth Henry, whose Whig husband had put her out of the house, was one such. Another was Elizabeth Gray, who was tried as a traitor and imprisoned "in a Dismal Dungeon" for ten months when she attempted to deliver a letter to General Burgoyne. A Philadelphia milliner named Margaret Hutchinson managed to pass in and out of the American camp at Valley Forge carrying "Severall Letters, at different times, of the greatest importance, besides Verbal Intelligence, of what, she had seen, of their different Movements." Ann Bates, who taught school in Philadelphia before the war, has been called "the most successful female spy in history." She was certainly an ingenious gatherer of military intelligence. She posed as a peddler and passed in and out of the American camp with a supply of "Rhuberb, Thread,

Needles, Combs, Knives &c." Women selling such
goods were common in the army and she attracted no
attention. As she later reported when applying for a
British pension, "I then Divided my little Stock in
Different lots as near as I could form an Idea of their
Number of Brigades allowing one lot for Sale in Each
Brigade, by which means I had the Opportunity of going
through their whole Army remarking at the same time
the strength & Situation of each Brigade, & the Numbers
of Cannon with their Situation and Weight of Ball each
Cannon was charged with." The Patriots became suspi-
cious of her a few times, but she was never caught.

The Loyalist woman whose activities were potentially
of greatest value to the British may have been Margaret
Shippen Arnold of Philadelphia. In 1779, when she was
nineteen, she married a thirty-eight-year-old Patriot
general named Benedict Arnold. Within a month of this
marriage, General Arnold, who had performed heroically
for the Patriots at Ticonderoga, Quebec, and Saratoga,
had decided to defect to the British. It seems probable
that his new wife, who was a devoted Loyalist, had a good
deal to do with his decision. Taking advantage of the
upper-class convention that discounted the importance of
women's political views, Margaret Shippen Arnold had
cultivated gentlemen friends on both sides of the conflict.
She approached one of her Patriot friends, the New York
Congressman Robert R. Livingston, and persuaded him
to get her husband assigned to the command of West

Point. At the same time she put her husband in contact with Major John André, a British officer she had been friendly with during the occupation of Philadelphia. She remained in the thick of the plotting as Arnold and André arranged to deliver West Point to the British. The scheme was foiled at the last minute by the capture of Major André. General Arnold had to run for his life, leaving his wife and child behind to explain the situation to General Washington. Margaret Arnold pretended total ignorance and was convincing enough to persuade both Washington and Alexander Hamilton of her innocence. But a compromising letter from Major André addressed to her was shortly discovered. A Philadelphia newspaper declared that evidence should disprove "the fallacious and dangerous sentiments so frequently avowed in this city that female opinions are of no consequence in public matters . . . Behold the consequence!" Mrs. Arnold joined her husband in exile.

The most flamboyant woman Loyalist was probably Flora McDonald. She seems at first glance a most unlikely person to take the British side. Thirty years earlier, in her native Scotland, she had participated in a revolt against England. She was at the Battle of Culloden and was responsible for saving the life of "Bonnie Prince Charlie." As a result of this activity Flora McDonald was imprisoned by the British in the Tower of London. After her release, she and her husband, like many other politically undesirable Highlanders, emigrated to the colony of North Carolina. One would think they would have been glad to join the Patriots during the Revolution. After the Battle of Culloden, however, the defeated Scottish rebels had been required to take an oath of allegiance to the English king. The Presbyterian Scots took such oaths very seriously. Because they had given their oath that they would remain loyal, the North Carolina Scots could not support the Patriots. The Patriots would not tolerate their remaining neutral. So Flora McDonald and her family took part once again in a revolt against England; but this time they were Loyalists rather than rebels. Her husband was a major in the Loyalist North Carolina militia, her son was a captain, and her son-in-law was a colonel. She herself, however, was the best-known and most conspicuous of her clan. In 1776 she accompanied her husband as he rode from house to house recruiting a Loyalist force. When his troops were ready to march out, she addressed them in Gaelic and reviewed the men while mounted on a white horse. Nine days later this Loyalist force was defeated at the Battle of Moore's Creek. Her husband was imprisoned and his property confiscated. Flora McDonald and her four children took passage for Scotland. During the voyage a French privateer attacked the ship. Flora McDonald encouraged the sailors to resist the attack and suffered a broken arm during the engagement. This courageous and colorful woman finally reached Scotland safely. She never returned to America.

Exile was probably less painful for new immigrants like Flora McDonald than it was for the tens of thousands of native-born Americans who were also forced to leave their homes as a result of their Loyalism. There were probably half a million more or less dedicated Loyalists in a total American population of two and a half million. Most of these remained in America keeping quiet and so escaping notice or somehow winning the forgiveness of their neighbors. But between 80,000 and 100,000 Loyalists became permanent exiles as a result of the war. These refugees were a truly pitiable group. Most of the hardships of war were shared by both sides. Patriot women as well as Loyalist lost relatives in the fighting, had their property destroyed or stolen, were abused by hostile soldiers, and had to worry about providing for their children in a war-torn country. But when the fighting was over Patriot women could feel that their sufferings were somehow worthwhile. Their side had won. Loyalist women, however, who were unable to return to their homes and were offered very little support from the British government, were left feeling defeated and bitter.

At the time, of course, the Patriots had no sympathy for their defeated enemies. They regarded those Americans who had sided with the British as the worst of traitors. Thus in April, 1776, one year after the battles of Lexington and Concord, Abigail Adams wrote, "We have intelligence of the arrival of some of the Tory fleet at Halifax, that they are much distressed for want of houses, obliged to give six dollars per month for one room, provisions scarce and dear. Some of them with six or eight children round them sitting upon the rocks crying, not knowing where to lay their heads. Just Heaven has given them to taste of the same cup of affliction which they one year ago administered with such callous hearts to thousands of their fellow citizens, but with this difference that they fly from their injured and enraged country, whilst pity and commiseration received the sufferers whom they inhumanely drove from their dwellings." She could hardly be expected to be more compassionate. Bostonians still remembered the events of April, 1775, when "British troops unmolested and unprovoked wantonly and in a most inhuman manner fired upon and killed a number of our contrymen, then robbed them of their provisions, ransaked plundered and burnt their houses! Nor could the tears of defenseless women, some of whom were in the pains of childbirth, . . . appease their thirst for blood or divert them from their design of murder and robbery." They remembered how "women in childbed were driven by the soldiery naked into the streets . . . and such scenes exhibited as would disgrace the annals of the most uncivilized nation." Thus they would have no pity for those Americans who had refused to oppose King George and his troops.

With the perspective of history, however, we can see that war meant brutality on both sides. Many of the women Abigail Adams saw crying on the rocks had probably been goaded into opposition to the Patriots by some atrocity committed by the Sons of Liberty. Others who found themselves driven from their homes probably had no understanding at all of the political issues involved in the war. Perhaps the greatest use of history is that it teaches compassion for both sides and especially compassion for ordinary people caught up in great events.

Consider the story of Hannah Ingraham, who was perhaps a typical Loyalist refugee. She was just a baby when the fighting began. Her family had a comfortable farm twenty miles north of Albany, New York. Her father, like many New Yorkers, had no sympathy for the New England rebels, and he joined the British army. He served for seven years. For four of those years Hannah's mother had no news from him and did not even know whether he was alive. When her father left, the local Patriots confiscated the farm. They allowed the family to continue to live there, but they had to pay rent. Mrs. Ingraham was allowed to keep four sheep and one heifer, and when Hannah's four-year-old brother tearfully begged to keep his pet lamb the Patriot soldiers left that too. Everything else was taken. When the war was over, Benjamin Ingraham came home to his family and told them they would have to leave the country. They would go, he said, to Nova Scotia.

Years later Hannah remembered the trip made when she was eleven. They killed the heifer — now grown to a cow, sold its meat, and made candles from the tallow. An uncle threshed twenty bushels of wheat and their grandmother made bags to hold it. The family packed their clothing and household utensils and then set off for their new home with the wheat, the candles, "a tub of butter, a tub of pickles, and a good store of potatoes." They went down the Hudson River in a sloop. At New York City they transferred their belongings onto a British transport called the *King George*. Hannah remembered that several babies were born on the ship during the voyage to Canada.

There was a bad storm in progress when they arrived. The family had to live in tents provided by the British government. "It was just at the first snow," Hannah remembered, "and the melting snow and rain would soak up into our beds as we lay. Mother got chilled and developed rheumatism and was never well afterwards." Benjamin Ingraham worked to build his family a new house while they slept in the tent and the winter grew colder. Finally, a great day: "One morning when we awoke we found the snow lying deep on the ground all round us and then father came wading through it and told us the house was ready and not to stop to light a fire and not to mind the weather, but follow his tracks through the trees, for the trees were so many we soon lost sight of him going up the hill. It was snowing fast and oh, so cold. Father carried a chest and we all took something and followed him up the hill through the trees to see our gable end." At the new house they found "no floor laid, no windows, no chimney, no door, but we had a roof at least. A good fire was blazing and mother had a big loaf of bread and she boiled a kettle of water and put a good piece of butter in a pewter bowl. We toasted the bread and all sat around the bowl and ate our breakfast that morning and mother said: 'Thank God we are no longer in dread of having shots fired through our house. This is the sweetest meal I ever tasted for many a day.' "

Not all refugees accepted their exile so cheerfully. Sarah Frost kept a diary in which she described her voyage to Canada. She sailed on a ship called the *Two Sisters,* which was part of a convoy of fourteen vessels accompanied by a British warship. Conditions were extremely crowded; seven families shared the cabin Mrs. Frost and her children were in. The crowding didn't help people's tempers and there was a good deal of quarreling. The children were uncomfortable and there were a great many of them. "We bear with it pretty well through the day," Sarah Frost wrote, "but as it grows toward night one child cries in one place and one in another, whilst we are getting them to bed. I think sometimes I shall be crazy." To make things worse, an epidemic of measles broke out. When, after two weeks, Mrs. Frost and her children were able to go ashore she wrote in her diary, "It is, I think, the roughest land I ever saw." Another woman exile recalled her feelings as she saw the convoy of ships that had brought them to Canada sailing away: "I climbed to the top of Chipman's Hill and watched the sails disappearing in the distance, and such a feeling of loneliness came over me that, although I had not shed a single tear through all the war, I sat down on the damp moss with my baby in my lap and cried."

Few of the Loyalist exiles had lived in such primitive frontier conditions in their homes in America. To be transported to a northern wilderness where snow was at times six feet deep and to live in a tent was very hard on women who were used to a well-kept farm or a comfortable house in town. The shock was especially profound for those who came from southern colonies. It was many years before such women could forget the homes they had left behind and start looking forward. It was easier for children. In 1860 an old woman who had been a little girl in a Loyalist refugee family could look back on those early days as happy times: "The Country at that time was a complete wilderness but by energy and perseverance and a long time we got on very happily . . . Mother used to help to chop down Trees, attended the household duties, and, as the children grew up, they were trained to Industrious habits. We were very useful to her, attended the cattle, churned the butter, making cheese, dressing the flax, spinning, (in those days the spinning-wheel looked cheerful), made our own cloth and stockings . . . The Bay of Quinte was covered with Ducks of which we could obtain any quantity from the Indians. As to fish, they could be had by fishing with a scoup. I have often speared large Salmon with a pitchfork. Now and then provisions ran very scant, but there being plenty of Bull frogs we fared sumptuously . . . We had no Doctors, no Lawyers, No stated Clergy . . . An old woman in the next clearing was the Chief Phys[i]cian to the surrounding Country as it gradually settled."

About half of the Loyalists exiled from America during and after the Revolution ended up in Canada, primarily in Nova Scotia and Quebec. This was the case with most of those who spent the war years in England as well as those who did not leave America until the war was lost. A good number of southern Loyalists fled to Florida during the war. But the British returned Florida to Spain after the war, and the Loyalists had to move again. Some went back to the United States. Others went to Canada or to England. The largest number went to the Bahamas or other islands in the Caribbean. Wyannie Malone, a Loyalist woman who left her home in South Carolina in 1785, ended up on a tiny isolated island called Hopetown. In 1903 an American scientific expedition discovered a colony of white inhabitants on Hopetown. Almost all of them were descendants of Wyannie Malone. They had preferred incest to miscegenation. As a result of extreme inbreeding for over one hundred and fifty years, a horrifying number of them were idiots, dwarfs, and victims of other generic diseases and deformities.

In general, however, the sufferings of the Loyalists did

not last beyond one generation. The great majority of exiles prospered in their new homes. Indeed these hard-working American refugees laid the foundations of British prosperity in Canada and the Bahamas.

7

DAUGHTERS OF LIBERTY

ORGANIZATIONS of women appeared in America as early as the seventeenth century. The tendency of women to form "circles" or "clubs" has continued into the present day. It is one of the central themes in American women's history. In the nineteenth century, middle-class women's organizations usually confined themselves to ladylike charitable activity or study groups devoted to self-improvement. Colonial women, however, who had not yet learned to be ladies, organized clubs that concentrated on political discussion and activity.

Perhaps the original impetus behind the formation of women's organizations in colonial times was the nature of

women's work. The constant spinning, knitting, and
sewing kept the hands busy but left the mind free. In any
community where women had neighbors living within a
few miles, and certainly in the towns, they would arrange
to do such work together. It was only natural that the
conversation in such groups would turn to political and
economic matters. When public affairs were at a critical
point or struck at the economic and business interests of
the women, politics might well take precedence over
sewing. In this way formal women's organizations were
born.

The first formal women's organization that we know
of was holding regular business meetings in Burlington,
New Jersey, in 1681. In 1707 a Charleston, South
Carolina, physician reported that "the women of the
town are turned politicians also and have a club where
they meet weekly among themselves." By 1733 there
was an organization of businesswomen in New York
City who published a political protest in the *New York
Journal*: "We the widows of this city, have had a
Meeting, and as our case is something Deplorable, we beg
you will give it Place in Your Weekly *Journal*, that we
may be relieved, it is as follows: We are House Keepers,
Pay our Taxes, carry on Trade and most of us are she
Merchants, and as we in some measure contribute to the
Support of Government, we ought to be entitled to some
of the Sweets of it; but we find ourselves entirely
neglected, while the Husbands that live in our Neighbor-

hood are daily invited to Dine at [the English governor's] Court; we have the vanity to think we can be full as Entertaining, and make as brave a Defence in Case of an Invasion and perhaps not turn Taile so soon as some of them." Two years later, in 1735, New York City had a "large company of agreeable women between the ages of fifteen and fifty" who met every Tuesday. These were formal meetings, regulated by a presiding officer, who was seated in a "great chair" just as was the presiding officer of the colonial legislature.

The devotion of women's circles to serious issues and formal organizational structure did not lead to the abandonment of the spinning and sewing activity that had brought women together in the first place. Indeed, there came to be a strong connection between spinning and politics. In the eighteenth century, cloth manufacture was England's most important industry. The colonies were discouraged from producing any manufactured goods of their own and always suffered from an unfavorable balance of trade with the mother country. When American women spun and wove their own cloth, imports from England could be reduced. Frugality and self-sufficiency of this sort strengthened the colonial economy and so was a patriotic activity. Furthermore, reducing the American market for English cloth could be a method of economic warfare. When colonial women responded to an unpopular English law by increasing their spinning, they could hope to cause unemployment and social disturbances in the English cloth-manufacturing districts. Such domestic troubles would put pressure on the English Parliament to repeal the objectionable legislation.

Women understood the political uses of spinning long before the American Revolution. In 1748 three hundred "young female spinsters" in Boston formed "The Boston Society for the Promoting of Industry and Frugality." On one occasion they held a political rally on Boston Common, bringing their spinning wheels and working spools of flax for a full day. This action was sufficiently impressive to be mentioned in the British Parliament. When the Stamp Act crisis developed in 1765, signaling the beginning of the Revolutionary era, women were as quick to respond as were the men. As Patriot men began to refer to themselves as "sons of liberty," Patriot women called themselves "daughters of liberty." Both began to organize in 1766.

The first meeting of a women's organization using the name "Daughters of Liberty" is said to have been in Providence, Rhode Island. Similar groups, however, appeared spontaneously in all parts of America. At times they used the term "daughters of liberty," at other times they identified themselves only as an "Association of Ladies." A New England minister praised the spinners for undertaking work by which "the women might recover to the Country the full free Enjoyment of all our rights, Properties & Priveleges (which is more than the Men have been able to do." Throughout the pre-Revolutionary years, American women clearly viewed their spinning wheels as weapons. Every piece of disturbing news was apt to be met by women plying their wheels with increased energy. Thus a traveler in New Jersey in 1768 reported, "At another gentleman's house where I was, his lady was spinning fast, and had five clever girls spinning along with her ever since they heard that the Boston Parliament was dissolved."

The diary of Abigail Foote, a young girl from Colchester, Connecticut, vividly illustrates how individual women fit some patriotic — what Abigail calls "Nationly" — activity into their very busy lives. Here, in its entirety, is Abigail's entry for one day in 1775: "Fix'd Gown for Prude Just to clear my teeth, — Mend Mother's Riding-hood, — Ague in my face, — Ellen was spark'd last night, — Mother spun short thread, — Fix'd two Gowns for Welch's girls, — Carded tow — spun linen — worked on Cheese Basket, — Hatchel'd Flax with Hannah and we did 51 lb a piece, — Pleated and ironed, — Read a sermon of Dodridge's, — Spooled a piece — milked the cows — spun linen and did 50 knots — made a broom of Guenea wheat straw, — Spun thread to whiten, — Went to Mr. Otis's and made them a swinging visit, — Israel said I might ride his jade, — Set a red Dye, — Prude stayed at home and learned Eve's Dream by heart, — Had two scholars from Mrs. Taylor's

— *I carded two pounds of whole wool and felt Nationly,*
— spun harness twine, — scoured the Pewter." (Italics
added.)

Since cloth was England's major industry, the boycott
of textiles was thought to be the most important economic weapon that could be used against the mother
country. Well-to-do women, who were accustomed to
dress in imported cloth, took pride in wearing homespun
purchased locally. Boycotts of other imports, however,
were also instituted by the Patriots. Women merchants
as well as men signed nonimportation agreements. Members of women's groups pledged to abstain from the use of
imported luxury items, especially those bearing a contro-
versial tax.

Taxation was a prime issue in the pre-Revolutionary
debate. The Townshend duties of 1767 were an attempt
to raise revenue for England without the consent of the
colonial legislatures. They constituted an import tax on a
variety of items important to the colonists. These
included lead, paint, glass, paper, and tea. The American
nonimportation agreements eventually caused enough
hardship in England to persuade Parliament to repeal all
but one of the Townshend duties. The tax on tea was
retained as a symbol of what the Parliament claimed was
its right to levy such taxes. Tea thus became a symbol for
Americans too. Abstention from tea became mandatory
for all true sons and daughters of liberty. Since women

bore the primary responsibility for putting food and drink on the table, the tea boycott became uniquely a woman's cause.

Tea was a hard thing to give up. It was usually the first luxury item purchased by an American family when it had a bit of cash to spare. Relatively few people cared for coffee and cola drinks were unknown. Tea was thus not only a delicious drink in itself but the center of those pleasant social occasions that today center around coffee cups or sodas. Americans were extraordinarily fond of it. But they were fonder of their right to self-government. Women's anti-tea leagues sprang up to compliment the spinning societies. Women pledged to give up tea themselves, encouraged others to renounce it, and devised ingenious substitute "liberty teas" to make the abstinence less painful. Women experimented with brews of various local leaves including sassafras, sage, strawberry, raspberry, and currant. A brew made from the red-root bush was known as Labradore tea. Probably many women served one of the medicinal teas from their books of recipes. At any rate an Englishman who received a sample of "liberty tea" from America declared it had "a very physical taste." Nevertheless, daughters of liberty were warmly encouraged to proceed with their activities as in this piece of verse, which was widely reprinted:

First, then, throw aside your topknots of pride,
Wear none but your own country linen,

Of Economy boast, let your pride be the most,
To show clothes of your own make and spinning.

What if home-spun, they say, is not quite so gay
As brocades, yet be not in a passion,
For when once it is known, this is much worn in town,
One and all will cry out—" 'Tis the fashion"

Throw aside your Bohea and your Green Hyson tea
And all things with a new-fashion duty;
Procure a good store of the choice Labrador[e]
For there'll soon be enough here to suit ye;

These do without fear, and to all you'll appear
Fair, charming, true, lovely, and clever,
Tho' the times remain darkish, young men may be sparkish,
And love you much stronger than ever.

In January, 1770, five hundred and thirty-eight Boston
women "in which number the Ladies of the highest rank
and influence that could be waited upon in so short a time
are included" signed an agreement vowing not to drink
tea so long as it was taxed. After Parliament passed the
Tea Act in 1773, compounding the injury of the
Townshend tax by encouraging an East India Company
monopoly, organized resistance to tea drinking became
even stronger in America. The newspapers were filled
with reports of women's anti-tea activities, holding each
good example up to women in other localities as worthy
of emulation. For instance, the Newport, Rhode Island,

newspaper of December 20, 1773, carried this item: "We
can assure the Publick, that a Lady in this Town, of
affluent Circumstances, and equal to any One in it for
good Sense, Politeness and Consequence, last Week
came to the Resolution to have no India Tea drank in her
Family until the Duty upon that Article is taken off; and
Example well worthy the Imitation of every Individual in
the Colony, and throughout the Continent." A few days
later a newspaper in Williamsburg, Virginia, reported,
"By Letters from Boston, we hear that the Ladies of that
Place, to their Immortal Honour, have entered into an
Association against the Use of East India Tea; and they
intend sending their Compliments soon to all other
Ladies on the Continent to refrain from that Baneful
Practice, at least till America is freed from Parliamentary
Taxation."

In this way women acted themselves and at the same
time signaled encouragement to their sisters in distant
parts of the country. In July, 1769, the *Virginia Gazette*
declared with "greatest pleasure" that the "Association of
Ladies meets with the greatest encouragement in every
county that we have yet heard from." Five years later
the same paper was carrying notices to Virginia women
from their "sisters and countrywomen" in South Carolina
and messages directed to the "Dear Ladies" of Pennsylvania urging American women everywhere to abstain
from "all luxuries, especially Tea."

The best-known of the women's anti-tea declarations

is that signed in Edenton, North Carolina, in October, 1774, shortly after the meeting of the First Continental Congress. Fifty-one women attended a meeting at the home of Elizabeth King and adopted a declaration that read in part, "As we cannot be indifferent on any occasion that appears to affect the peace and happiness of our country, and as it has been thought necessary for the publick good to enter into several particular resolves, by meeting of the Members of Deputies from the whole Province, it is a duty that we owe not only to our near and dear relations and connections, but to ourselves who are essentially interested in their welfare, to do everything so far as lies in our power to testify our sincere adherence to the same, and we do therefore accordingly subscribe this paper as a witness to our fixed intentions and solemn determination to do so." They vowed to give up the "Pernicious Custom of Drinking Tea" and also not to "promote the wear of any Manufacture from England until such time that all Acts which tend to Enslave this our native Country shall be repealed."

The English, who did not encourage political activity by ladies, found the notion of a women's convention very amusing. They ridiculed the Edenton meeting as the "Edenton Tea Party." A cartoon was produced and sold showing the Edenton women signing the declaration and emptying their tea canisters. Most of the women, especially the presiding officer, are extremely ugly. The most attractive member of the group is nuzzled by a young man, presumably a Patriot, as she takes up the pen to sign. A black woman holds the inkwell while a baby girl and a dog upset a tray of cakes under the table. A copy of this cartoon was sent to the North Carolina Patriot James Iredell from London by an English correspondent who remarked, "I see by the newspapers the Edenton ladies have signalized themselves by their protest against tea drinking . . . Is there a female Congress at Edenton too? I hope not, for we Englishmen are afraid of the Male Congress, but if the ladies . . . should attack us, the most fatal consequence is to be dreaded . . . the only security on our side to prevent the impending ruin, that I can perceive, is the probability that there are but few places in America which possess so much female artillery as Edenton."

This gentleman was, of course, quite wrong. When war broke out American women demonstrated, both in their individual actions and in their organized efforts, that they were as fully involved in the cause as the men. "Be it known unto Britain," wrote Mercy Otis Warren, "even American daughters are politicians and patriots, and will aid the good work." The women of America produced a swarm of colorful heroines who, but for the prejudices of traditional historians, would be as well known as Paul Revere or Nathan Hale. Since they were ignored by scholars who did not feel women's stories were "real" history, the record of their exploits was until recently kept only in family oral traditions. As a result

even that part of women's history that was preserved
became overladen with myth.

A prime example of a real woman whose true
contributions to the American war effort have been
concealed and distorted by folklore is Betsy Ross. Betsy
Ross is probably the best-known woman of the entire
Revolutionary generation. But she is known for something she did not do. The story we all know describes a
committee of the Continental Congress, made up of
George Washington, Robert Morris, and George Ross,
which was appointed to design a flag for the new United
States. They are said to have produced a sketch of what
they wanted, which featured six-pointed stars. When
they called on Mrs. Ross and asked her to sew up a flag
based on their design she persuaded them to substitute
five pointed stars by demonstrating how easily she could
cut out such a star with one snip of the scissors. Some
versions of the story say that the committee was so
pleased with the flag she produced that they gave her a
contract and she continued to be official flagmaker for the
American government for the rest of her life. This story
was first told publicly in 1870 by Betsy Ross's grandson.
It was so charming a tale that it was picked up and
reprinted in *Harper's Monthly* and then in school text-
books. Charles H. Weisberger produced a painting
called *Birth of our Nation's Flag* which showed Mrs. Ross
displaying her five-pointed star flag to the members of the
Congressional committee. Before the end of the century

there was a Betsy Ross Memorial Association raising money to convert the Philadelphia house where the event was said to have taken place into a national shrine. Two million schoolchildren and members of patriotic society each donated a dime for the "Flag House," and received a copy of the Weisberger painting in return. Unfortunately, there is no substance to the Betsy Ross legend.

Betsy Ross lost two husbands in the Revolution, the first while he was on militia duty in January, 1776, and the second when he died in an English prison after being captured at sea. Her first husband, John Ross, had been apprenticed to an upholsterer and she herself had been trained in needlework. When the war began they had an upholstery shop in Philadelphia. As a widow, Mrs. Ross did supplement her income by making flags. But these were not made for Congress. The evidence shows that she was paid a sum in May, 1777, for making "ship's colours, &c." for the Pennsylvania State Navy Board. The Continental Congress never appointed a flag committee. The Flag Resolution adopted by Congress on June 14, 1777, left considerable latitude to flag designers. It specified only that there be thirteen stripes, red and white, and thirteen stars in a blue field. It said nothing about how many points the stars should have, their arrangement, or the arrangement of the stripes. Authorities now believe that the first "stars and stripes" flag used by American forces was the "Bennington Flag." That banner has an arch of eleven seven-pointed stars over the numerals "76" with two additional stars in the top corners of the field.

Betsy Ross, then, did not make the first American flag. But at least her name has been remembered. The stories of hundreds of other women, both truer and more dramatic are still to be brought to public attention. A fine example is the story of Sybil Ludington of Fredericksburg, New York. Her nighttime ride to arouse the countryside of the approaching British was at least as bold and as successful as a more famous ride made two years earlier by a Bostonian named Paul Revere.

Sybil Ludington was the sixteen-year-old daughter of Colonel Henry Ludington, who commanded a Patriot militia unit. On the evening of April 26, 1777, an exhausted messenger arrived at the Ludington home announcing that the British were raiding Danbury, just across the state line in Connecticut. Danbury was a Patriot supply center guarded by fewer than two hundred Continental troops. They were under attack by two thousand British and Loyalist troops. Colonel Ludington's men were urgently needed.

During the Revolution, the local militia units operated as a volunteer fire brigade might today. They did not live in barracks but in their own homes scattered over a wide area. Someone must ride through the night and carry the word to the militiamen that they must turn out. Sybil Ludington did the job. Mounted on her horse Star and carrying a stick in her hand, she rode forty miles through the dark countryside, banging on the doors of the houses as she passed. Those who answered Paul Revere's call had not saved Concord, and the men who turned out that night were not in time to save Danbury. Sybil Ludington, however, did successfully complete her mission while Paul Revere was captured during his midnight ride. Her father's troops were able eventually to force the British to retreat back to their ships in Long Island Sound.

The stories of women who participated in the military activities of the war are mentioned in Chapter 8. Women's civilian support activities were just as important, however, if less dramatic. The American Revolution is the only war the United States has ever fought in which there was not a pool of unemployed or underemployed women to take up the slack when men were recruited into the army. To keep the army supplied and to keep the civilian population from starving, women and children had to work longer hours and cut down their own consumption of food and clothing. They were never able to keep the Patriot armies supplied as well as the British, but this was not the result of indifference. There were limits to how much a full-employment economy could increase production when the British and American armies destroyed homes and farms and when men left their productive jobs for military occupations.

The outbreak of fighting in April, 1775, led first to an increase in the same activities daughters of liberty had undertaken in earlier stages of the conflict. Now that clothing for soldiers was needed, women's spinning became more essential than ever. The *Pennsylvania Magazine* noted in December, 1775, "While the men defend our borders and cultivate our land, the women must not neglect what is proper in their sphere . . . As we must furnish clothing for many thousands more than we have heretofore done, the Spinning Wheel requires their particular attention . . . There are at least 600,000 females in these Thirteen Colonies, of an age sufficient to spin." A well-to-do woman, who had not earlier participated in the tea boycott or worked herself to produce clothing at home, became active in these ways after the fighting began. In a letter to a British officer she wrote, "I will tell you what I have done. My only brother, I have sent to the camp with my prayers . . . and had I twenty sons and brothers they should go. I have retrenched every superfluous expense in my table and family; tea I have not drunk since last Christmas, nor bought a new cap or gown since your defeat at Lexington; and what I never did before, have learned to knit, and am now making stockings of American wool for my servants; . . . I know this — that as free, I can die but once: . . . these are the sentiments of all my sister Americans."

The outbreak of war provided additional opportunities for women's participation. Those who were trained in occupations that could be useful to the war effort brought their talents to the support of the Patriot cause. Betsy Ross and those like her produced the regimental banners and other flags necessary to military units that practiced the European drill and fought in formal European style. Other women tanned goat skins to make drumheads, also necessary to well-disciplined units. Guns were needed both by trained units and by the local militia groups that fought as guerillas. Gunsmiths like Catherine Smith and blacksmiths like Elizabeth Hager helped provide these weapons. Women with a talent for writing could be sure that no one would remind them that ladies were not supposed to participate in political controversy if they used their pens effectively in support of the Patriot cause.

A number of women wrote pieces for the newspapers during the war. Anne Stockton of Pennsylvania produced a series of poems on liberty. Phillis Wheatley wrote a poem in honor of General Washington, which was published in the *Pennsylvania Magazine* in April, 1776. Ann Terrell of Virginia wrote a piece entitled "The Ladies whose Husbands are in the Continental Army" in which she declared that when she thought about America's grievances she was ready to take up a sword herself and fight beside her husband. A writer using the name "Belinda" wrote to the editor of *The New Jersey Gazette* in 1778, "I do not remember whether your *Gazette* has hitherto given us the production of any woman correspondent — Indeed nothing but the most pressing call of my country could have induced me to appear in print. But rather than suffer your sex to be caught by the bait of that arch foe to American Liberty, Lord North, I think ours ought, to a woman, to draw their pens, and enter our solemn protest against it."

The most prominent female propagandist for the Patriot cause was Mercy Otis Warren. Her father, husband, and brother were all active Patriots and her home in Plymouth, Massachusetts, was the scene of frequent political meetings. She became an active propagandist in 1772, when she published a play entitled *The Adulateur*. Playacting was not permitted in Boston; Mrs. Warren never saw a stage production in her life. But she admired the satire of the French playwright Molière, whom she had read. Her plays were only written to be read. *The Adulateur* was followed by *The Defeat, The Group, The Blockheads,* and *The Motley Assembly.* In all of these easily recognizable local Loyalists appear under such names as Rapatio, Judge Meagre, Sir Spendall, and Hum Humbug. These pieces stung the Loyalists and delighted the Patriots. When Mrs. Warren, who had read many of the "ladies' books" wondered to John Adams whether her activity was altogether proper, he sprang to reassure her. Politics was not inappropriate for Patriot women, he said, and Mrs. Warren had "a Share and no Small one neither, in the Conduct of our American Affairs."

In addition to the activities of individual women,

women's organizations continued to support the Patriot cause after the war began. They coordinated the production of stockings for soldiers and cloth for army uniforms. They distributed the recipe for saltpetre and prepared quantities of that substance, which is essential to the manufacture of gunpowder. They held scrap drives, and collected everything from pewter dishes and forks to fishnet weights to be melted down into shot. Some women's groups even manufactured cartridges. A group in Litchfield, Connecticut, got hold of most of a statue of George III that had been pulled down from New York's Bowling Green by the Sons of Liberty. They melted down the lead, poured it into molds, and then wrapped each bullet in oiled paper with the right amount of gunpowder for a musket charge. General Oliver Wolcott recorded that the group produced 42,088 cartridges. Finally, women's groups might use their influence to encourage men to enlist in the army. "The young ladies of the best families of Mecklenburg County" in North Carolina publicly declared that they would not keep company with any young gentleman who had not done military service. The young ladies of Rowan County quickly followed this example. Their resolutions were entered in the minutes of the Patriot Committee of Safety and declared "worthy the imitation of every young lady in America." In New Jersey it was reported that "the fair ones in our neighborhood have already entered into a resolve for every mother to disown her son, and refuse the caresses of her husband, and every maiden to reject the addresses of her gallant," if these men wavered in their devotion to the cause.

The largest of the women's wartime organizations was known simply as the "Association." It was founded in Philadelphia in May, 1780, under the leadership of Esther Reed, wife of Pennsylvania Governor Joseph Reed. The Association was conceived as a national organization, coordinated by governors' wives and Martha Washington. Its purpose was to raise money to be distributed as a special gift of gratitude to the Continental troops, an "offering of the Ladies." There is evidence of Association activity in Maryland, New Jersey, Delaware, Virginia, and South Carolina as well as in Pennsylvania. Although it is impossible to estimate how many women may have worked with the Association, it was unquestionably the largest organization of American women up to that time and for at least half a century afterward.

The Association distributed a broadside entitled *The Sentiments of an American Woman.* It included a rousing essay citing the wartime achievements of women from Deborah and Judith to Joan of Arc and Catherine of Russia together with the Association's plan of operation. All contributions would be accepted, "the shilling offered by the Widow or the young Girl . . . as well as the most considerable sums." Women in each county were to designate a "Treasuress" who would collect from the local canvassers and then forward the money to the state

"Treasuress-General," the Governor's wife. The total
collected in each state would finally be sent to Mrs.
Washington or to General Washington should his wife
not be at the camp. These funds could be spent in
whatever way General Washington believed would be
"most advantageous to the Soldiery." The only condition
was that it not be spent for basic rations, clothing, or
weapons: "It is an extraordinary bounty intended to
render the condition of the Soldiery more pleasant, and
not to hold place of the things which they ought to
receive from the Congress or from the States."

American women responded enthusiastically to this
call. In rural areas the local churches coordinated the
drive. In the towns women canvassed from house to
house. The canvassers covered the city of Philadelphia
systematically. They did not "let the meanest ale house
escape." The list of contributors records donations of
women in all ranks of society from servants to the wives
of generals. The subscription list tells us of a "Widow
Fox" who gave eight Continental dollars, of "Polly Fritz,
a little girl" who gave five Continental dollars, of the
anonymous "Miss Nobody" who gave one hundred and
fifty paper dollars and the anonymous "Miss Somebody"
who gave eight dollars in gold. A certain Mrs. Richards
donated "a pair of leather breeches" which were sold for
a thousand Continental dollars, and Mrs. Robert Morris,
wife of the man known as the "Financier of the
Revolution," donated her time to the canvass and put in

ten thousand dollars of her own. Within a few months the women of Philadelphia alone had raised the equivalent of $7500 in gold. This was in a time of fierce inflation. A single gold dollar was equivalent to forty Continental dollars. The sum raised by the Philadelphia women was only a few hundred dollars less than prominent business-men in the city were able to raise in their simultaneous drive to establish a Bank of the United States.

The leaders of the Association wanted to make a cash gift to every Continental soldier, but General Washing-ton discouraged this idea. He told Mrs. Reed, "I have my apprehensions (from the peculiar circumstances of our Army) that a taste of hard money may be productive of much discontent, as we have none but depreciated paper for their pay . . . it will be the means of bringing punishment on a number of others whose propensity to drinking . . . leads them to irregularities and disorder which must be corrected." The women agreed to substitute a gift of shirts. Mrs. Reed had begun to purchase linen for the shirts and arrange for the sewing when she died suddenly in September, 1780, at the age of thirty-four.

After Mrs. Reed's death a five-member committee took over the direction of the Association. Sarah Bache, Benjamin Franklin's daughter, was one member. The others were Henrietta Bonde Hillegas, Anne Willing Francis, Mary Bonde Clarkson, and Susan Blair. In the fall of 1780 a French visitor to Mrs. Bache's home was shown "into a room, filled with needlework, recently finished by the ladies of Philadelphia. This work consisted of . . . shirts for the soldiers . . . On each shirt was the name of the married or unmarried lady who made it, and there were 2,200 shirts in all." In December, 1780, these shirts were distributed among the most needy soldiers in the Continental Line.

Esther Reed's project to raise army morale by a gift to the soldiers apparently inspired her husband to plan a similar gift for the women with the army the following year. He tried to persuade the Executive Council of Pennsylvania to fund the scheme: "A new gown, silk handkerchief, and a pair of shoes, etc., would be but little expense, and I think as a present from the State would have more effect than ten times the same laid out in articles for the men." If the government would not fund the project, however, Joseph Reed said he would "be one of a hundred to provide for one woman each, to be given only to those soldiers' wives who continue in the service." Unlike his wife's plan, however, Joseph Reed's scheme was never implemented.

The support of the daughters of liberty must have been deeply appreciated by the ragged men in the American camps. At a time when neither Congress nor the state governments had been able to provide the troops with adequate clothing, the organized efforts of American women stepped into the gap. General Washington sent the leaders of the Association a formal letter of thanks:

"The army ought not to regret their sacrifices or sufferings, when they meet with so flattering a reward as the sympathy of your sex; nor can they fear that their interests will be neglected, while espoused by advocates as powerful as they are amiable."

8

WOMEN AND WAR

WﾐAR AND VIOLENCE were endemic in colonial America. Mob violence and riots were regular occurrences both in the towns and in the countryside. War between English, French, and native Americans raged along the whole North American frontier with few interruptions throughout the eighteenth century. These conditions accustomed Americans of both sexes to the use of weapons. The nineteenth-century "lady," who fainted at the sight of blood and was too kindhearted to swat a mosquito, had no place a century earlier. For their own survival, colonial women learned to threaten force and to kill in self-defense. Even in the towns respectable matrons could behave with a ferocity that would be thought shockingly improper if not impossible for females a generation later.

Every colonial home had its weapons, although contrary to common belief, there was not a rifle or even a musket over every colonial American's fireplace. Guns were expensive, required an expert to keep in repair, and were slow to load. Consequently, while some civilians owned muskets, blunderbusses, or squirrel guns, many more looked to axes, hoes, scythes, and similar domestic implements as weapons to be used in an emergency. On the frontier, where settlers learned to expect attack without formal warning, the records are full of descriptions of feminine proficiency at arms. Consider this incident, which took place in the Shenandoah area of Virginia in 1766: Two families were traveling by wagon toward a fort during an Indian alert. They were attacked by five Indians and both men were killed. "The women," we are told, "instead of swooning at the sight of their bleeding, expiring husbands, seized their axes, and with Amazonian firmness, and strength almost superhuman, defended themselves and children. One of the Indians had succeeded in getting hold of one of Mrs. Sheetz's children, and attempted to drag it out of the wagon, but with the quickness of lightning she caught her child in one hand, and with the other made a blow at the head of the fellow, which caused him to quit his hold to save his life. Several of the Indians received pretty sore wounds in this desperate conflict, and all at last ran off, leaving the two women with their children to pursue their way to the fort." Or again, consider the case of Mrs. Mack, who was living alone with her children in a wilderness cabin. One evening when she went outside to get some corn for dinner she heard a noise and realized that Indians were about. She walked carefully back inside the cabin, put the children to bed hungry, and sat up all night with a loaded gun. Just before dawn an Indian slipped into the cabin through the chimney and attacked Mrs. Mack with a tomahawk. She shot him dead and then killed three of his companions who were waiting outside. Mrs. Mack and her children then started for the fort where Mr. Mack was stationed and finally reached safety after killing another party of Indian attackers on the way. Similar tales abound.

In the towns, the use of violence by popular mobs was an accepted feature of political life in the predemocratic era when most people could not vote. Women as well as men launched physical attacks in order to determine some public policy. In 1677, during King Philip's War, the people of Marblehead, Massachusetts, who had suffered considerably from Indian attacks, were enraged when two Indian captives were taken alive rather than killed. One of the men responsible for the capture reported that a mob of Marblehead women "laid violent hands upon the captives, some stoning us in the meantime, because we would protect them, others seizing them by the hair,

got full possession of them . . . Then with stones, billets
of wood, and what else they might, they made an end of
these Indians . . . They cried out and said, if the Indians
had been carried to Boston, that would have been the end
of it, and they would have been set at liberty; but said
they if there had been forty of the best Indians in the
country here, they would have killed them all, though
they should be hanged for it. They suffered neither
constable nor mandrake, nor any other person to come
near them, until they had finished their bloody purpose."
Thirty years later a female mob in Boston assaulted the
troops returning from an unsuccessful Canadian expedition during Queen Anne's War with the contents of
chamber pots.

In the years before the Revolution, and during the war
itself, mobs made up of daughters of liberty used force to
prevent merchants from stocking British goods or from
hoarding and to intimidate Loyalists. Or, with less
patriotic motives, a female mob might appropriate some
staple commodity that was reserved for the army in time
of need. In East Hartford, Connecticut, for instance, the
newspaper reported in the fall of 1777 that "a large corps
of female infantry, of 20 rank and file . . . marching
westward about one mile, in martial array and excellent
order . . . there attacked and carried without opposition
from powder, law or conscience, Mr. Perkin's store in
which was lodged a quantity of sugar designed for the
army of which they plundered and bord away in triumph

218 lb." A man who attempted to follow them and who was taken for the offending shopkeeper "was attacked . . . with great fury." But, the newspaper explained, since he was on horseback and the women were on foot, he managed to escape.

About the same time Abigail Adams described a similar episode in Boston: "One eminent, wealthy, stingy merchant (who is a bachelor) had a hogshead of coffee in his store, which he refused to sell the committee under six shillings per pound. A number of females, some say a hundred, some say more, assembled with a cart and trunks, marched down to the warehouse, and demanded the keys, which he refused to deliver. Upon which one of them seized him by his neck and tossed him into the cart. Upon his finding no quarter, he delivered the keys when they tipped up the cart and discharged him; then opened the warehouse, hoisted out the coffee themselves, put it into trunks and drove off."

Patriot women, as well as men, were known to believe that tar and feathers was the appropriate clothing for Tories of either sex. A Virginia newspaper reported that a mob of almost two hundred New England women set out to tar and feather the mother of a newborn baby who had been christened Thomas Gage, in honor of the military governor of Massachusetts. According to the report, "only the pleas of the distracted father restrained the mob." In another incident the wife and fifteen-year-old daughter of a Boston man who had accepted an ensign's commission from the British were tarred and feathered by a mob of women, "disregarding their goodness, beauty, and embarrassment."

When the military conflict began, in April, 1775, it was expected that women would participate. In addition to sporadic mob activities, women saw combat in three roles: as campfollowers with the Continental troops, as regular soldiers who disguised their sex, and as irregular fighters on the frontier affiliated with local militia units.

Nineteenth-century historians, reading the practices of the Victorian era back into the eighteenth century, casually assumed that the campfollowers of the American Revolution were prostitutes. They seem to have felt that the only way to handle the thousands of females who accompanied the army was to ignore them or, at best, to give them a few sentences in which they refer vaguely to women of "vicious character." Consequently, while every schoolchild is reminded of the hardships of American men at Valley Forge, the many women who suffered for the Patriot cause at least as much as the men they followed are totally blacked out of history or else casually slandered.

Let it be made quite clear that in eighteenth-century America the term "campfollower" was by no means a synonym for whore. Today the campfollowers would be called WACs, or field nurses, or army wives. They were respectable married women, frequently pregnant and usually accompanied by their children, who were recog-

nized as an essential part of the military organization.
They were not treated equally with the male troops —
they traveled with the baggage and received only half
rations — but their contribution to the military effort was
recognized by officers and men on both sides. Campfollowers had served with the regular troops in all the wars
with French and Indians in the eighteenth century.
Women who had served in many campaigns viewed their
army life as a career just as their husbands did. This
attitude is illustrated by a petition sent by an army wife to
the commander of her husband's regiment after she had
been put in jail for using abusive language to an officer: "I
have been a Wife 22 years to have traveld with my
Husband every Place or Country the Company marcht
too and have workt very hard ever since I was in the
Army. I hope yr Honour will be so good as to Pardon
me this onct time that I may go with my Poor Husband
one time more to carry him and my good Officers water
in ye Hottest Battle as I have done before. Yr unfortunate Petitioner and Humble Servant, Martha May."

The British armies brought some soldiers' wives with
them from England, Ireland, and Germany. During the
War, many British and Hessian troops married American
women who followed them in the army. It appears that
the number of women with the British approximately
doubled between 1777 and 1781. The English soldiers
eventually had one woman for every one and a half men

and the German mercenaries had one woman for every fifteen men.

Just as soldiers in the regular armies of Europe were recruited from a level of society so debased that it had no counterpart in the New World, so the wives of the British soldiers appeared so wretched that they shocked the Americans. Many were abandoned far from home when it was inconvenient for the British to transport them with the army. Others stuck with their men even after the officers cut off their rations and they were forced to live on what their husbands could spare. A Boston woman left this description of the women with the army captured by the Americans at Saratoga in 1777: "I never had the least Idea that the Creation produced such a sordid set of creatures in human Figure — poor, dirty, emaciated men, great numbers of women, who seemed to be the beasts of burden, having a bushel basket on their back, by which they were bent double, the contents deemed to be Pots and Kettles, various sorts of Furniture, children peeping thro' gridirons and other utensils, some very young infants who were born on the road, the women bare feet, cloathed in dirty rags, such effluvia filld the air while they were passing, had they not been smoking all the time, I should have been apprehensive of being contaminated by them." These unfortunate women, who were rarely provided for adequately from the army stores, became a special scourge to the civilian population, whether Loyalist or Patriot, in every area the British army passed through. It was said they took particular pleasure in stealing from and insulting the civilian women who lived in the comfortable little cottages and farmhouses along the line of march.

In the early days of the war there was a great shortage of women on the Patriot side. As the war progressed the number of women with the American army increased. It would appear, however, that there were never as many women with the American armies as with the British.

Most of the American soldiers joined Washington's army at least partly for economic reasons. It is probable that most women also had economic motives for joining. As the movements of the British troops made refugees of civilians, women who could not support themselves and their families when deprived of a husband's assistance in farm or shop, found the campfollower's stipend extremely attractive. The American army provided the women who worked for the troops with half rations for themselves and quarter rations for each child. There was no such thing as a dependent's allowance in eighteenth-century armies. Only women who actually accompanied the troops were allowed to share army rations. In 1779, when a number of wives whose husbands were on an expedition into the Indian country where, it was well known, women and children were in special danger, applied to be allowed to draw rations while remaining at West Point, General Washington refused. "This is a thing which I have never known to be allowed," he wrote, "and which, if admitted in one instance, might be claimed by the families of the whole Army."

If a woman who wished to march with the army did not have a husband to follow or if her husband should be killed, the American army was liberally provided with chaplains to help her form a new connection. At the same time, the American officers, who prided themselves on their moral superiority to the "corrupt" British, took good care that no "lewd women" appeared in camp. As early as June, 1776, Colonel Israel Hutchinson, who was in command of Dorchester after the siege of Boston, ordered inspection of the women "that the Wheat may be selected from the Tares (if any be found)." But the inspectors found only legitimate wives and children.

Eventually there were so many refugees following the army that General Washington found them a burden. They slowed the movements of the army dangerously. In August, 1777, as Washington was attempting to maneuver his army to protect Philadelphia from the invading army of General Howe without risking capture himself he issued the following order: "In the present marching state of the army, every incumbrance proves greatly prejudicial to the service; the multitude of women in particular, especially those who are pregnant, or have children, are a clog upon every movement. The Commander in Chief therefore earnestly recommends it to the officers commanding brigades and corps, to use every reasonable method in their power to get rid of all such as are not absolutely necessary; and the admission or continuance of any, who shall, or may have come to the army since its arrival in Pennsylvania, is positively forbidden, to which point the officers will give particular attention." A few weeks later, as an engagement seemed imminent, it was ordered that "every species of baggage . . . will now be stored . . . women are expressly forbid any longer, under any license at all, to ride in the waggons, and the Officers earnestly called upon to permit no more than are absolutely necessary, and such as are actually useful, to follow the army."

Washington was, however, very reluctant to order wives to leave the army even when the proportion of women to men went well over the one to fifteen ratio authorized by the Continental Congress. He believed that many of his best troops would desert if their families were abandoned. Furthermore, the services of the camp-followers were essential.

In an age when infection and disease killed far more soldiers than enemy bullets, the traditional women's work — feeding the men, nursing them, and keeping them clean — was not expendable to an army. Few men were trained in these "womanly" skills. In the early days of the war, before many women had joined the troops, it was almost impossible to maintain minimum standards of hygiene in the American camp. "Many of the Americans have sickened and died of the dysentery," wrote an observer during the siege of Boston, "brought upon them in a great measure through an inattention to cleanliness. When at home, their female relations put them upon washing their hands and faces, and keeping themselves neat and clean; but, being absent from such monitors, through an indolent, heedless turn of mind, they have neglected the means of health, have grown filthy, and poisoned their constitution by nastiness."

A year later, when Congress sent a committee to Ticonderoga to report on conditions there, an inspection of the hospital at Fort George revealed that there were four hundred sick and wounded soldiers who "suffered much for Want of good female Nurses." It should be remembered, however, that the eighteenth century considered too much cleanliness unwholesome. When Washington ordered that the troops should have time off to bathe every Friday afternoon, he also stipulated that no man was to be permitted to spend more than ten minutes in the water.

Campfollowers were also essential to maintain the clothing of the troops. Just as shirts and stockings were unavailable to the army at any price unless women at home would take on the extra work required to produce them, shirts and stockings quickly turned to rags without women with the troops to repair them. Contemporary observers felt that much of the ragged, unkempt appearance of the American army was due to their having an insufficient number of women to wash and mend. "Not

being used to doing things of this sort," wrote one man,
the American soldiers "choose rather to let their linen,
etc., rot upon their backs than to be at the trouble of
cleaning 'em themselves."

Although most of the campfollowers, like most of the
Continental troops, came from the lower class, campfol-
lowing was not confined to poor women. Officers' wives
also followed the flag. Martha Washington boasted that
she had heard the first and last gun of every campaign of
the war although she only joined her husband in camp
and did not go along the line of march. Rebecca Biddle
and Kitty Greene were also found at camp. Lucy Knox,
wife of General Henry Knox, did accompany her
husband on the march and was said to follow the camp
fire as certainly as the drum.

On the British side, some officers clung to their
prerogatives as "gentlemen" by taking mistresses. The
most notorious was General William Howe's mistress,
Mrs. Loring, who was known as "the sultana." She and
Sir William spent three years of campaigning together,
making the best of army life by spending a good deal of
time drinking and gambling. Patriots sneered at the
British general's gallantry and attributed his failure to
launch a decisive attack against the American army on his
fondness for his paramour. As one wit expressed it:

> *Sir William, he, snug as a flee,*
> *Lay all this time a-snoring,*

Nor dream'd of harm as he lay warm
In bed with Mrs. Loring.

Not all British officers, of course, indulged in such scandalous behavior. Most seem to have been satisfied with the wives who followed them accompanied by ladies' maids, cooks, and stores of wine and delicacies. The highest ranking campfollower was probably Baroness von Riedesel, wife of the Hessian general. She came to America to meet her husband, bringing their three small daughters, all under five. She bore a fourth child, named America, during the war. For six years the Baroness traveled with her husband in a private coach together with two maids and the children. She kept a detailed journal that provides the sharpest picture available of the life of an upper-class Revolutionary War campfollower.

The presence of upper-class ladies in camp made it possible for officers of both sides to continue some semblance of civilized life. Gambling and conversation were possible without ladies, but the dancing that was so popular among colonial aristocrats was not. An attempt by French officers to teach the gavotte and quadrille to Indian women at some of the desolate outposts during the French and Indian War had not been notably successful. General Washington was exceedingly fond of dancing. We have record of him dancing with Mrs. Greene "upwards of three hours without once sitting down" at what General Greene described as "a pretty little frisk" in March, 1779, and dancing with Lucy Knox, the plump wife of General Henry Knox in May, 1782. A newspaper reported Washington's "dignified and graceful air," as the couple "carried down a dance of twenty couple in the arbor on the green grass."

Although the living conditions of upper-class campfollowers were superior to those of their poorer sisters — just as the officers lived better than the enlisted men — they were not idle parasites on camp supplies. Although they were not sent out to forage for horses or to clean the barracks, they did mend uniforms, sew shirts, knit stockings, and assemble baskets of food and home remedies for sick soldiers. In an emergency such a woman might also supervise a field hospital. She might also aid in such clerical chores as copying enclosures for letters or transcribing file copies of outgoing communications. The services such women performed usually won them the gratitude and admiration of the troops as persons in their own right, not merely as ornamental wives to their officers.

All eighteenth-century armies had camp duties that were regularly assigned to women. Campfollowers also had a role to play during battle. They were the primary medics, carrying water and tending the wounded. Their memory survives under the generic name Molly Pitcher. The original Molly Pitcher is usually identified as either Margaret Corbin or Mary Hays. Those women were typical of others who, in the heat of battle, naturally moved from carrying water (which was needed to swab out the cannon after each firing) to carrying powder and shot and from that to loading and firing muskets or field pieces. Eighteenth-century women were used to handling weapons, and when they saw a job that needed doing they did not wait for a man's help; they did it themselves.

Margaret Corbin was born in Pennsylvania in 1751. She learned of war early in life; her father was killed and her mother captured during an Indian raid when Margaret was five. She was raised by an uncle and married John Corbin about 1772. When her husband enlisted as an artillery private at the outbreak of the Revolution, Margaret Corbin became a campfollower. The incident for which she earned a place in history (although it was largely unrecognized during her lifetime) took place during the defense of Fort Washington on Manhattan Island in November, 1776. Her husband was stationed at a small cannon in an exposed position. He was killed and Margaret took over his place. Shortly after she too was seriously wounded; one of her arms was almost severed and a breast was badly lacerated by grapeshot. She remained an invalid for the rest of her life, living on charity in the Invalid Regiment until 1783 and then on a small Congressional pension. She lived until about 1800 and was known in the village of Highland Falls, New York, where she settled as "Captain Molly," a bad-tempered, hard-drinking eccentric. Although she was buried in an unmarked grave, her story was handed down through oral tradition. In 1926, the sesquicentennial of Independence, Margaret Corbin was reburied at West Point, and a monument was erected in her honor.

Mary Hays made her reputation at the battle of Monmouth in June, 1778. The daughter of a dairy farmer, she went to work as a domestic at the age of thirteen and married a barber named William Hays the same year. William enlisted as a gunner in the Pennsylvania artillery when the war began and Mary eventually joined him at camp in New Jersey. The legend describes her as taking over her husband's position at the Battle of Monmouth after he was wounded. The one contemporary eyewitness, however, describes both husband and wife as working together: "A woman whose husband belonged to the artillery and who was then attached to a piece in the engagement, attended with her husband at the piece the whole time. While in the act of reaching a cartridge and having one of her feet as far before the other as she could stemp, a cannon shot from the enemey passed directly between her legs without doing any other damage than carrying away all the lower part of her petticoat. Looking at it with apparent unconcern, she observed that it was lucky it did not pass a little higher, for in that case it might have carried away something else, and continued her occupation." It is noteworthy that this observer is struck by Mrs. Hays's coolness under fire rather than by her presence on the battlefield.

After the Revolution Mary and her husband returned to Pennsylvania. After his death she married John McCauley, another veteran of the Revolution. She continued to work as a domestic for private families and as a charwoman in the Carlisle courthouse. In 1822 she was awarded a pension by the Pennsylvania legislature. Like Margaret Corbin, however, she received no special recognition for her military activity during the Revolution until long after her death. A special marker was not placed on her grave until 1876.

Margaret Corbin, Mary Hays, and the many other campfollowers who took up arms in the heat of battle, fought as women. They wore their usual skirts and petticoats and expected no pay except for the campfollower's half-ration. Other women, however, sought the full pay, rations, and recruitment bounty due to regular soldiers by disguising themselves as men and enlisting in the ranks.

We do not know just how many women soldiers served in the Revolution. Only a handful who were discovered or had some reason for revealing their secret later in life have left any record. During the Civil War, three quarters of a century later, several hundred women soldiers were discovered, some having served as long as two years before their true sex was revealed. Certainly it would have been even easier for a woman to pass as a man in the Revolutionary army.

The Continental army was so desperate for troops that recruiters would accept almost anyone who was willing to enlist. They accepted runaway slaves and servants and boys as young as eleven or twelve. A young woman who bandaged her bosom need not fear arousing suspicion by the pitch of her voice or the lack of a beard. The constant tending of a kitchen fire, which was a normal feminine duty, and the use of lye soap gave most women red rough complexions at an early age. Their faces would certainly rasp as hard as those of teenaged boys. Furthermore, many men used the woods instead of the latrines. They slept in their clothing and seldom bathed. Unless a woman soldier was wounded or became ill she had a good chance of avoiding discovery.

The few women we know of for certain who succeeded in enlisting as men include a Creole girl, Sally St. Clair, who was killed in the war, and a Massachusetts woman who rose to the rank of sergeant under the name of Samuel Gay before she was discovered and discharged from the service. The best known of the male impersonators in the Revolutionary army is Deborah Sampson Gannett. She was born in Massachusetts and at the age of ten was bound out as a house servant. She learned the appropriate domestic skills during this apprenticeship and also got enough education at a local school to enable her to become a teacher herself after her term of service was up. She apparently had an adventuresome spirit and a taste for travel and the bounties being offered to soldiers tempted her. In April, 1781, at the age of twenty, she enlisted in the Continental army under the name of Robert Shurtleff. She performed her duties well and was present at the final battle at Yorktown. Although she was wounded in a skirmish at Tarrytown, New York, she managed to keep her secret until she fell ill with a fever. Then a surgeon discovered her secret and she was discharged in October, 1783. After the war she married Benjamin Gannett, a Massachusetts farmer, and had three children. She won fame in her own lifetime, unlike Margaret Corbin and Mary Hays, because she decided to capitalize on her wartime experiences. In 1797 she became the first American woman to go on the lecture circuit. She always remained poor, however, and held pensions both from the State of Massachusetts and from the Federal Congress. After her death, Congress granted her husband a pension recognizing him as the widower of a Revolutionary soldier.

On the American frontier, the Revolutionary War was but one part of the prolonged warfare between Native Americans and white settlers. It was in this part of the war and in resistance to attacks by small parties of British troops or Loyalist militia that most American women were touched by the violence of the Revolution. Just as many men who would not join the Continental army served bravely with local militia units or Committees of

Safety, so many women who would not leave their homes
to follow the army would nevertheless fight to defend
those homes when attacked. In Groton, Massachusetts,
for instance, when Mrs. Wright and Mrs. Shattuck
learned that the British were coming, they organized a
female militia. The women dressed in men's clothing,
took up what muskets, pitchforks, or other weapons they
could lay hands on, and succeeded in dispersing a British
detachment at Jewetts Bridge. In upper New York, Mrs.
Elizabeth Petrie Shell fought to defend her cabin when it
was attacked by Indians and Loyalist militia. She loaded
guns for her husband and sons. When the enemy pressed
so close to the cabin that they could push their guns
through chinks in the wall, she took up an axe and
smashed the barrels. Another New York woman, Nancy
Van Alstyne, became so renowned as an Indian fighter
that she was known as "Patriot Mother" of the Mohawk
Valley. The name was particularly appropriate as Mrs.
Van Alstyne had borne fifteen children. Loyalist women
also participated in the irregular warfare of the Revolution. In September, 1777, a party of Loyalists was jailed
in Poughkeepsie, New York. The band was "charged
with robbing several houses and putting the families in
fear . . . they were all painted and dressed like Indian
men . . . five of them proved to be women, three of
whom are a mother and two daughters."

In hundreds of encounters such as these, American
women participated in the war for American independ-

ence. They were more fully engaged in the military activity of this war than they would be in any other war the United States has ever fought. Their active participation was due partly to the irregular character of the war in which there was no clear division between war zone and homefront. It was partly due to the shortage of manpower, which made discrimination against women in any kind of work impractical. And it was partly due to the failure of the English "ladylike" ideal to take root in America, so that a woman who shed blood was not exposed to criticism or self-doubts.

Most of the women who fought in the Revolution probably did so primarily for immediate motives of self-defense or economic necessity. So did most of the men. But once having been drawn into the war, some, at least, came to understand and identify with the larger principles for which the war was fought. And a few Americans of both sexes even glimpsed the feminist implications of the Revolutionary demands for freedom and equality.

9

THE AMERICAN REVOLUTION
AND THE RIGHTS OF WOMEN

THE SLOGANS of the American Revolution that declared the rights of liberty and self-determination to be self-evident implied an attack on the inequality of the sexes. In 1848, when the Seneca Falls Convention adopted the Declaration of Sentiments that is recognized as the beginning of the nineteenth-century feminist movement, it was written as a paraphrase of the Declaration of Independence. The theorists of the Revolution certainly did not anticipate that their arguments would be extended so far. Yet their doctrines were contagious. Whatever their intent, the Revolutionary doctrines were extended to justify social democracy, the abolition of slavery, the separation of church and state, and, eventually, equal legal and political rights for women.

"No taxation without representation!" was a fundamental demand of the Patriots from the earliest days of the Revolutionary crisis. The conclusion was inescapable that women who paid taxes should have the right to vote. Of course very few women in the colonial period paid taxes. Married women, who were the vast majority, could not hold legal title to property. Any taxes due were paid by the husband. Unmarried girls from wealthy families could not hold title to property until they were of age, and once they came of age they almost always were married. Spinsters were rarely wealthy enough to owe taxes, and widows usually remarried so quickly that few of them were taxpayers on more than one election day. Yet the principle requiring that taxpayers have the right to consent to legislation affecting their pocketbooks was so firmly established in America that only three states — Pennsylvania, Delaware, and South Carolina — had laws disfranchising women who otherwise met the property and residence requirements for voters.

Although they were theoretically entitled to vote, there are only isolated instances of women casting ballots before the Revolution. Even among the tiny number of women whose ownership of property and absence of a marital tie qualified them, the right to vote was seldom exercised. For most of the eighteenth century, however, the rate of political participation was very low even among men who were qualified to vote. Taxpayers felt it was important that their colonial legislatures, not Parliament, vote on taxes. But most taxpayers had so much respect for their wealthy neighbors that they were content to let them decide who would sit in the legislature. Because it was so uncommon for a woman to vote, it is probable that most women who qualified were unaware that voting was their legal right. In 1777, Hannah Lee Corbin of Virginia wrote to her brother Richard Henry Lee urging him to support giving the suffrage to widows. She pointed out that they did pay taxes and it was unfair to impose taxation without representation. He replied that he "would at any time give my consent to establish their right of voting" but in fact they already had "as legal a right to vote as any other person." Nevertheless, there are a mere handful of examples of women voting in Virginia and obviously none of them were acquaintances of Mrs. Corbin. Lee speculated that the wealthy widows who would qualify as voters may have stayed away from the polling places in order to guard their ladylike image. Certainly the English ladies described by the ladies' books were not voters. "Perhaps 'twas thought rather out of character for women to press into those tumultuous assemblages of men where the business of choosing representatives is conducted," he told his sister.

A year before Hannah Lee Corbin wrote her letter claiming the right to vote, John Adams and James

Sullivan had been discussing the claims of women to the franchise. They, like Mrs. Corbin, seem to have been unaware that New England women theoretically could demand voting rights and that a small number had actually exercised them. "It is certain, in theory, that the only moral foundation of government is, the consent of the people," Adams wrote. "But to what extent shall we carry this principle? Shall we say that every individual of the community, old and young, male and female, as well as rich and poor, must consent . . . Depend upon it, Sir, it is dangerous to open so fruitful a source of controversy and altercation . . . there will be no end of it. New claims will arise; women will demand a vote; lads from twelve to twenty-one will think their rights not enough attended to; and every man who has not a farthing, will demand an equal voice with any other, in all acts of state." Adams seems to have predicted the long-range impact of the Revolutionary ideology accurately enough.

Two days before the Continental Congress adopted the Declaration of Independence, the state of New Jersey adopted a new constitution that put the Revolutionary doctrine of consent into practice. "All inhabitants of this Colony, of full age, who are worth fifty pounds proclamation money, clear estate in the same and have resided within the county in which they claim their vote, for twelve months immediately preceding the election, shall be entitled to vote . . ." In case there was any doubt that this law meant what it said, the New Jersey

Legislature adopted an election law in 1790 that explicitly referred to voters by the words "he and she." Unmarried women, now fully aware of their rights, then went to the polls in New Jersey in significant numbers for almost twenty years. In some townships it was said they cast a quarter of the votes. In 1797 a Newark newspaper printed verses for a song entitled "The Freedom of Election" including this stanza:

> *What we read, in days of yore,*
> *   the woman's occupation,*
> *Was to direct the wheel and loom,*
> *   Not to direct the nation.*
> *This narrow minded policy*
> *   by us hath met detection;*
> *While woman's bound, man can't be free,*
> *   nor have a fair election.*

The entire electoral process in New Jersey, however, was extremely corrupt in the last years of the century. Those in charge at the polling places decided who to admit or exclude according to their own political views. In order to win an election wives as well as single women and an assortment of black slaves, servants, and young boys were allowed to register votes. Under these circumstances the women voters were not exercising any significant right, they were merely exploited. The abuses finally became so scandalous that the New Jersey Legislature acted in 1807 to restrict the suffrage to "free, white, male citizens" as was the practice in most of the other states. Free blacks as well as unmarried white women thus lost the rights that had been theirs under the Constitution of 1776.

Although voting rights became an important goal for the nineteenth-century feminist movement, the issue was unimportant for women of the Revolutionary generation. So long as most women married and the common law put wives under the absolute dominion of their husbands, reform of the common law was a far more vital goal than suffrage. The equality of women under the law, which was deliberately repudiated in the English legal tradition, was rarely suggested as a desirable goal. An exception was an anonymous poet in the *Virginia Gazette* of October 15, 1736 who wrote:

> *The Equal Laws let Custom find,*
> *And neither sex oppress;*
> *More freedom to Womankind*
> *Or give to Mankind less.*

Most critics of the common law did not suggest equality for wives but only some moderation of the virtually unlimited power husbands had over wives.

The common law had been relaxed considerably in America during the seventeenth century. Furthermore, pioneer conditions and the absence of courts and lawyers made it possible for women to exercise more freedom than they were legally entitled to. In the eighteenth century, however, a legal reaction set in which reached its culmination with the publication of Blackstone's *Commentaries*. This work was published in four volumes between 1765 and 1769. It was such a convenient summary of the law of England and America that lawyers embraced it eagerly. In the colonies, particularly, where books were scarce, every lawyer was soon using Blackstone as the final authority on every question. Unfortunately, Blackstone was very unkind to women. Far from having equal rights with men, married women were not even considered persons. The power of husbands was virtually absolute.

The impact of Blackstone's work was beginning to be felt in America in the years just before the Revolution. It occurred to some people that if America became independent of England a new legal system would have to be devised to replace the common law. Abigail Adams was one who thought independence would present an opportunity to reform some of the undesirable features in the English system. While she never suggested that wives should be equal to husbands, she did feel some moderation of husbands' rights would be in order. In March of 1776 she deliberately dropped a hint to her own husband, who was a member of the Continental Congress: "By the way in the new Code of Laws which I suppose it will be necessary for you to make I desire you would Remember the Ladies, and be more generous and favourable to them than your ancestors. Do not put such unlimited power into the hands of the Husbands. Remember all Men would be tyrants if they could." A fundamental belief of eighteenth-century political theorists was that "power corrupts." And Americans were aware of how power without limitation had made a tyrant of King George III. Abigail Adams drew the parallel closer as she continued her letter: "If perticuliar care and attention is not paid to the Laidies we are determined to foment a Rebelion, and will not hold ourselves bound by any Laws in which we have no voice, or Representation." She was not disturbed by the superiority of husbands over wives, only by the lack of limitation on their power. "That your Sex are Naturally Tyrannical is a Truth so thoroughly established as to admit of no dispute, but such of you as wish to be happy willingly give up the harsh title of Master for the more tender and endearing one of Friend. Why then, not put it out of the power of the vicious and the Lawless to use us with cruelty and indignity with impunity. Men of Sense in all Ages abhor those customs which treat us only as the vassals of your Sex. Regard us then as Beings placed by providence under your protection and in immitation of the Supreem Being make use of that power only for our happiness."

The Continental Congress, however, had no plans to overhaul the common law and Abigail Adams' plea for the ladies was so unexpected that it made her husband laugh. "As to your extraordinary Code of Laws," he wrote back to her, "I cannot but laugh. We have been told that our Struggle has loosened the bands of Government everywhere. That Children and Apprentices were disobedient — that schools and Colledges were grown turbulent — that Indians slighted their Guardians and Negroes grew insolent to their Masters. But your Letter was the first Intimation that another Tribe more numerous and powerful than all the rest were grown discontented . . . Depend upon it, We know better than to repeal our Masculine systems. Altho they are in full Force, you know they are little more than Theory. We dare not exert our Power in its full Latitude. We are obliged to go fair, and softly, and in Practice you know We are the subjects. We have only the Name of Masters, and rather than give up this, which would compleatly subject Us to the Despotism of the Peticoat, I hope General Washington, and all our brave Heroes would fight. I am sure every good Politician would plot."

Mrs. Adams was not too pleased by this response, "I can not say that I think you are very generous to the Ladies, for whilst you are proclaiming peace and good will to Men, Emancipating all Nations, you insist upon retaining an absolute power over Wives." But she did not press the point. After all, she was an upper-class woman. The ladies' books taught that a woman who had trouble with her husband would have her way by acknowledging his superiority. Accordingly she concluded this exchange with her husband by quoting a bit of ladylike advice for wives: "Charm by accepting, by submitting sway/Yet have our Humor most when we obey."

When women like Mrs. Adams accepted the principle of male domination in the family and in society it did not mean that they accepted intellectual inferiority for women. Abigail Adams and other American women of her class as well as a large number of men in the Revolutionary generation strongly supported improved education for women. Here they parted company with the doctrines taught by some of the ladies' books. The English moralists frequently criticized the "bluestocking" or "learned lady." A woman who was as well educated as a man, they thought, was unnatural. Although a certain amount of reading, especially of the Bible, was appropriate, true intellectual equality was not only unattractive in a female but might damage her brain. One book offered for sale in the colonies conceded that women ought not "forswear knowledge nor make a vow of Stupidity" but they must not "pretend to commence Doctors." She should avoid such subjects as science or divinity for such studies "lie out of a Lady's Way: They fly up to the Head, and not only intoxicate weak Brains, but turn them." Early in the colonial period Governor Winthrop of Massachusetts recorded the sad story of a woman who went mad as a result of her intellectual pursuits. She had given "herself wholly to reading and writing and had written many books." The governor felt that "if she had attended her household affairs, and such things as belong to women, and not gone out of her way to meddle with such things as are proper for men, whose minds are stronger, etc., she had kept her wits, and might have improved them usefully and honorably in the place God had set her."

The threat of brain damage was not taken seriously by many people in America of the eighteenth century, however. There were too many women who had successfully mastered advanced subjects without any ill effects. Hannah Adams of Medfield, Massachusetts, recorded in her autobiography that she "was very desirous of learning the rudiments of Latin, Greek, geography and logic." Although she did not go to Harvard to pursue such studies, "some gentlemen who boarded at my father's offered to instruct me in these branches of learning gratis, and I pursued these studies with indescribable pleasure and avidity." Miss Adams became a respected scholar and historian. Mercy Otis Warren, another distinguished New England historian, was tutored together with her brother until it was time for him to go to college. Then, at home, she continued to study the same subjects he did. Even a college education was not absolutely impossible for a woman to acquire. In December, 1783, the President of Yale examined Miss Lucinda Foote in Latin and Greek. He certified that the twelve year old girl "has made commendable progress, giving the true meaning of passages in the *Æneid* of Virgil, the select orations of Cicero, and in the Greek testament, and that she is fully qualified, except in regard to sex, to be received as a pupil of the Freshman Class of Yale University." Far from condemning the girl for her boldness in aspiring to the education usually reserved to boys, President Stiles accepted Lucinda as his private pupil and she pursued the full course of study under his direction. Even in the South, where education was valued less highly than in Puritan New England, there were learned women. George Wythe, a leading legal scholar in Revolutionary Virginia, had learned his Greek from his mother who was said to have possessed "a perfect knowledge" of the language. Martha Laurens of South Carolina also taught her sons Greek. Americans encouraged this sort of serious study for those upper-class women who had the leisure and the inclination for reading. It prevented them from turning to the frivolous books that absorbed the attention of English ladies of fashion.

The serious rather than ornamental studies of upper-class American women marked them as less cultured and less aristocratic than their counterparts in England. A gentleman writing in 1781 explained, "The women of Connecticut are strictly virtuous and to be compared to the prude rather than the European polite lady. They are not permitted to read plays; cannot converse about whist, quadrille or operas; but will freely talk upon the subjects of history, geography, and mathematics. They are great causists and polemical divines; and I have known not a few of them so well schooled in Greek and Latin as often to put to the blush learned gentlemen." This criticism was well taken. The serious studies of upper-class American women left them educated but not cultured. Abigail Adams questioned the value of reading the work of the great French playwright Molière because she thought he did not point a sharp enough moral lesson. Mrs. Margaret Schuyler of New York believed "Shakespeare was a questionable author" and considered his plays "grossly familiar, and by no means to be compared to 'Cato.' " Since upper-class Americans were anxious to be considered the equals of aristocratic Europeans, the criticism that their ladies were uncultured began to be felt keenly in the decades just before the Revolution.

The first stage in responding to the criticism of prudery was for Americans to attempt to continue educating their upper-class women in serious subjects but to encourage them to conceal their learning. Dr. Fordyce's much admired *Sermons to Young Women* recommended that they even conceal their common sense. He declared that since a sharp intelligence was generally incompatible with "softness and delicacy" a young lady should be "careful in displaying your *good sense*. It will be thought you assume a superiority over the rest of the company. But if you happen to have any learning, keep it a profound secret, especially from the men, who generally look with a jealous and malignant eye on a woman of great parts and a cultivated understanding." John Adams gave similar advice to his ten-year-old daughter when he learned that his wife was teaching her the basics of Latin grammar: "I learned in a letter from your mamma, that you was learning the accidence. This will do you no hurt, my dear, though you must not tell many people of it, for it is scarcely reputable for young ladies to understand Latin and Greek."

The advocates of advanced education for women had to support a delicate balance in their arguments. Upper-class women must have some education in order to differentiate them from their lower-class sisters. As Mercy Otis Warren observed, "when the cultivation of the mind in the early part of life is neglected in either sex, we see ignorance, stupidity, and ferocity of manners equally conspicuous in both." Yet they must not be so taken up with their scholarly pursuits as to lose the taste for homemaking. They must not become totally absorbed with their domestic duties, either. And they certainly must not turn to novels or fashion magazines. This advice was harder to follow than Mercy Otis Warren and others like her were willing to admit. "The task is easy," said Mrs. Warren, "at the same time, to be pursuing some mental improvement and yet neglect none of the duties of domestic life, provided there is a methodical and uniform plan of conduct, united with an industrious mind. But how miserable must that woman be who, at the same time that she has both genius and taste for literary inquiry, can not cheerfully leave the pursuit to attend to the daily cares of the prudent housewife. Though not less to be pitied is she who is wholly immersed therein and has no higher ideas than those which confine her to the narrow circle of domestic attention. Yet a still more contemptible part of the sex are those whose lives are one uninterrupted scene of dissipation and folly."

In the middle of the eighteenth century, if upper-class Americans had to choose between learned ladies and ladies of fashion as models they would choose the former. Although they recognized that the latter were closer to the aristocratic ideal, even the wealthiest men in America could not afford to support women whose occupations and interests were entirely unproductive. Dr. Benjamin Rush, in a well-known essay entitled "Thoughts on Female Education" written in 1787, argued that "female education should be accomodated to the state of society, manners, and government of the country, in which it is conducted . . . the education of young ladies, in this country, should be conducted upon principles very different from what it is in Great Britain." He noted that it was necessary for even upper-class American women to work. Their husbands needed their assistance in their various occupations and the servant class was not so large as it was in England. Furthermore, it was generally necessary for women to educate their own children, and they could not educate sons properly unless they were educated themselves. Others who argued for improved education for women followed the same argument. For instance, Abigail Adams wrote to her husband, "If you complain of education in sons what shall I say of daughters who every day experience the want of it? With regard to the education of my own children I feel myself soon out of my depth, destitute in every part of education . . . If we mean to have heroes, statesmen, and philosophers, we should have learned women . . . If as much depends as it is allowed upon the early education of youth and the first principles which are instilled take the deepest root great benefit must arise from the literary accomplishments in women." And again, Thomas Jefferson, in describing the education he wanted for his daughter Patsy wrote in 1783 that what he planned was "considerably different from what I think would be most proper for her sex in any other country than America. I am obliged in it to extend my views beyond herself, and consider her as possibly at the head of a little family of her own. The chance that in marriage she will draw a blockhead I calculate at about fourteen to one, and of course that the education of her family will probably rest on her own ideas and direction without assistance. With the best poets and prosewriters I shall therefore combine a certain extent of reading in the graver sciences."

The rationale for allowing more serious education to American ladies than was considered proper for European ladies was that such education would make the Americans better wives and mothers. It was never considered as a means to elevate women to a status of equality within the family. Mercy Otis Warren emphasized that "we own the appointed subordination (perhaps for the sake of order in families)" even as she encouraged women not to "acknowledge such an inferiority as would check the ardour of our endeavors to equal in all mental accomplishments the most masculine heights."

In the years following the Revolution there was a good deal of writing and discussion on the subject of women's education. This is often described as "feminist" writing because it argues for the intellectual equality of women and encourages developing their minds. The term is probably misapplied, however, for these writers argued only for intellectual equality, never for social or legal equality. Nevertheless, they do present a view of women superior to that held in England in that period or in the United States during the nineteenth century. Judith Sargent Murray, for instance, wrote a series of essays over the pen name *Constantia* ten years before the publication of Mary Wollstonecraft's *Vindication of the Rights of Women*, which anticipated many of the themes of the radical Englishwoman's writing. *Constantia* was particularly critical of the ornamental education given to those upper-class girls whose parents wished them to become ladies of fashion. It was, she said, "an education which limits and confines . . . employments and recreations which naturally tend to enervate the body, and debilitate the mind." From their earliest years the prospective lady of fashion was "adorned with ribbons, and other gewgaws, dressed out like the ancient victims previous to a sacrifice, being taught . . . that the ornamenting our exteriour ought to be the principal object of our attention." No wonder men, who are spared this conditioning, appear to be intellectually superior! But that, she insisted, is only an apparent superiority. "Will it be said that the judgment of a male of two years old, is more sage than that of a female of the same age? I believe the reverse is generally observed to be true. But from that period what partiality! how is the one exalted, and the other depressed, by the contrary modes of education which are adopted! the one is taught to aspire, and the other is early confined and limited. As their years increase, the sister must be wholly domesticated, while the brother is led by the hand through all the flowery paths of science. Grant that their minds are by nature equal, yet who shall wonder at the *apparent* superiority, if indeed custom becomes *second nature*." *Constantia* does not, however, suggest that women are capable of playing an equal role with men in the family. The natural order, she agrees, requires that men be the heads of families and that women attend to the housework. "You are by nature formed for our protectors," she concludes, "Shield us then, we beseech you, from external evils, and in return we will transact *your* domestick affairs."

When Mary Wollstonecraft's book became available in Boston and Philadelphia bookshops in 1790, it was received very favorably. Although the book aroused fierce criticism in later years, it expressed opinions that were fairly common in America immediately after the Revolution. As Elizabeth Drinker, an upper-class Philadelphian, put it, "In many of her sentiments she [Wollstonecraft], as some of our friends say, speaks my mind . . ." Like the American writers on women's education, Mary Wollstonecraft emphasized that serious education rather than training as a lady of fashion would make a woman a better wife and mother. "Women, subjected by ignorance to their sensations," she wrote, "and only taught to look for happiness in love, refine on sensual feelings, and adopt metaphysical notions respecting that passion which leads them shamefully to neglect the duties of life." Her encouragement to women to consider themselves intellectually equal to men and to devote themselves to serious study made her work popular in American girls' schools. A pupil at one Philadelphia school prepared an address in praise of Mrs. Wollstonecraft for presentation at a public program. Another admirer of the English writer produced ten stanzas of verse for the *Phildelphia Minerva* concluding:

Let snarling critics frown
Their maxims I disown,
Their ways detest;
By Man, your tyrant lord,
Females, no more be aw'd
Let Freedom's sacred word
Inspire your breast
Women aloud rejoice,
Exalt thy feeble voice
In cheerful strain.
See Wollstonecraft, a friend
Your injured rights defend,
Wisdom her step attend,
The cause maintain.

During the last half of the eighteenth century, and especially after the Revolution, there was a steady growth in the educational opportunities open to upper-class girls. Neither girls nor boys had many opportunities for advanced education in earlier years. Reading, writing, and simple arithmetic were considered sufficient except for the very wealthy who could afford to teach their children subjects that were "ornamental" rather than useful. Such young ladies and gentlemen might learn spelling, geography, foreign languages, music, drawing, and dancing. But such education was a luxury. In the absence of professional schools for such occupations as law and medicine, "book-learning" was either a personal pleasure or an aristocratic affectation. So-called accomplishments were often acquired with the avowed purpose of moving up in society. For instance, a Pennsylvania teacher who advertised his willingness to teach young ladies "true spelling with the rules for pointing with propriety" clearly stated the value this study would have to them. He had, he said, "the honour to give the finishing stroke in education to several of the reputed fine accomplished ladies in New York, some of which were married within two, three or four years afterwards." As the colonies grew wealthier, larger numbers of parents sought to give such educational advantages to their daughters. Boarding schools for young ladies proliferated. Judith Sargent Murray and other educational reformers were delighted by this development. In an essay published in 1798 *Constantia* wrote, "Female academies are everywhere establishing and right pleasant is the appellation to my ear . . . I may be accused of enthusiasm; but such is my confidence in THE SEX that I expect to see our young women forming a new era in female history."

Ironically, the female academies that *Constantia* welcomed so gladly proved to support the training of ladies of fashion rather than the learned ladies that she and the other reformers hoped to encourage. The increasing wealth of Americans had finally made it possible for them to support a group of idle women as aristocratic Europeans did. The desire to be equal to Europeans soon overwhelmed any desire a few seriously scholarly women had to be the intellectual equals of men. And Europeans had a very poor opinion of learned ladies. It was more important for a lady to have elegant manners and wear fine clothes. Young American girls were quick to appreciate that fact. Miss Molly Tilghman wrote to her cousin, Miss Polly Pearce, "Wisdom says [beauty] is a fading flower, but fading as it is, it attracts more admiration than wit, goodness, or anything else in the world." Most people — male or female — found little pleasure in mastering Latin grammar. It was small wonder then that as young ladies found themselves with leisure time they turned to novels with such titles as *The Maid of Quality*, *The Petticoat Plotter*, or *The Cloister, or Amours of a Jesuit and a Nun*. Reading them was far more enjoyable than translating the New Testament from the Greek. As the wealth of Americans continued to increase, the desire to raise one's daughters as ladies penetrated down into the middle class. Fathers began to discover it was difficult to persuade daughters to master the old-fashioned skills associated with women's traditional work when they could hope that mastering some ladylike accomplishments would snare a wealthy husband who would support them in idleness. Many readers of the *Boston Evening Post* must have sympathized with the father who insisted that his wife keep first things first in educating their daughter in this piece of verse:

Prithee, good madam, let her first be able
To read a chapter truly in the Bible,
Make her expert and ready at her prayer
That God may keep her from the devil's snares;
Teach her what's useful, how to shun deluding
To roast, to toast, to boil and mix a pudding
To knit, to spin, to sew, to make or mend,
To scrub, to rub, to earn and not to spend,
I tell thee wife, once more, I'll have her bred
To book'ry, cookr'y, thimble, needle, thread
First teach her these, and then the pritty fool
Shall fig her crupper at a dancing school.

In the quarter century following the American Revolution a new ideal came to dominate the thinking of
American women. Increasing wealth, the disappearance
of hardships associated with the frontier, and the desire to
prove American society equal to that of Europe persuaded American women to cultivate the passivity and
gentility of European ladies in place of the strength and
bravery that they had valued in an earlier period. Of
course slave women, servants, the very poor, and those
who continued to push the frontier to the west could not
adopt the new ideal. But all those who could afford to do
so strove to become ladies, and most young girls preferred
the ideal of the "lady of fashion" to the serious, scholarly
"learned lady." When John Quincy Adams, son of John
and Abigail Adams, was of an age to look for a wife, he

could find no one comparable to his mother. He complained to her the girls he met were all "simpering" and "superficial" and did nothing but "dance and talk scandal." His mother sharply replied that if girls were frivolous it was because men liked them that way; they were "like clay in the hands of the artist — and may be molded to whatever form [men] please."

Abigail Adams was as unfair as her son in placing the blame for the change that had come over American women on one sex alone. Both men and women supported the movement to substitute "refinement" for the rugged pioneer manners of an earlier age. The strong, hard-working, independent women of the Revolutionary generation were quickly forgotten. In 1840 Charles Francis Adams, the grandson of John and Abigail Adams, could write, "The heroism of the females of the Revolution has gone from memory with the generation that witnessed it, and nothing, absolutely nothing remains upon the ear of the young of the present day." We are only now beginning to recover their history.

Suggestions for Further Reading

GENERAL

James, Edward T., Janet Wilson James and Paul S. Boyer, eds. *Notable American Women.* Cambridge, Mass.: Harvard University Press, 1971.

Leonard, Eugenie Andruss. *The Dear-Bought Heritage.* Philadelphia: University of Pennsylvania Press, 1965.

Leonard, Eugenie Andruss, Sophie Hutchinson Drinker, and Miriam Young Holden. *The American Woman in Colonial and Revolutionary Times, 1565-1800.* Philadelphia: University of Pennsylvania Press, 1962.

Spruill, Julia Cherry. *Women's Life and Work in the Southern Colonies.* New York: W. W. Norton, 1972.

Thompson, Roger. *Women in Stuart England and America: A Comparative Study.* London and Boston: Routledge & Kegan Paul, 1974.

WOMEN'S WORK: HOMEMAKING

Calhoun, Arthur W. *A Social History of the American Family from Colonial Times to the Present.* New York: Arno, 1961.

Demos, John. *A Little Commonwealth: Family Life in Plymouth Colony.* New York: Oxford University Press, 1970.

Earle, Alice Morse. *Home Life in Colonial Times.* Stockbridge, Mass.: Berkshire Traveller Press, 1974.

———. *Customs and Fashions in Old New England.* Rutland, Vt.: C. E. Tuttle, 1971.

Holliday, Carl. *Woman's Life in Colonial Days.* Williamstown, Mass.: Corner House, 1968.

Morgan, Edmund S. *Virginians at Home: Family Life in the Eighteenth Century.* Charlottesville, Va.: University Press of Virginia, 1963.

WOMEN'S WORK: MAKING MONEY

Chapin, Howard M. *Ann Franklin of Newport: Printer.* Cambridge, Mass.: 1924.

Dexter, Elizabeth A. *Colonial Women of Affairs.* 2nd rev. ed. Clifton, N. J.: Augustus M. Kelley, 1972.

———. *Career Women of America, 1776-1840.* Clifton, N. J.: Augustus M. Kelley, 1950.

WOMEN'S ROLE AND WOMEN'S RIGHTS

Adams Family Correspondence. L. H. Butterfield, ed., Cambridge, Mass.: Harvard University Press, 1973.

Benson, Mary S. *Women in Eighteenth Century America: A Study of Opinion and Social Usage.* New York: 1966.

De Pauw, Linda Grant. "Land of the Unfree: Legal Limitations on Liberty in Pre-Revolutionary America," *Maryland Historical Magazine,* LXVIII, 1973, pp. 355–368.

Field, Verna B. *Constantia.* Orono, Maine: University of Maine Press, 1931.

Fritz, Jean. *Cast for a Revolution.* Boston: Houghton Mifflin, 1972.

Morris, Richard B. "Women's Rights in Early American Law," *Studies in the History of American Law.* New York: Octagon Books, 1964.

Whitney, Janet P. *Abigail Adams.* Westport, Conn.: Greenwood Press, 1947.

Woody, Thomas. *A History of Women's Education in the United States.* New York: Octagon Books, 1966.

BLACK WOMEN

Brodie, Fawn M. *Thomas Jefferson: An Intimate History.* New York: W. W. Norton, 1974.

Felton, Harold W. *Mumbet: the Story of Elizabeth Freeman.* New York: Dodd, 1970.

Genovese, Eugene D. *Roll, Jordan, Roll: The World the Slaves Made.* New York: Pantheon, 1974.

Graham, Shirley. *The Story of Phillis Wheatley.* New York: Messner, 1949.

Mullin, Gerald W. *Flight and Rebellion: Slave Resistance in Eighteenth Century Virginia.* New York: Oxford University Press, 1972.

Wood, Peter H. *Black Majority: Negroes in Colonial South Carolina from 1670 through the Stono Rebellion.* New York: Knopf, 1974.

NATIVE AMERICAN WOMEN

Hodge, Frederick Webb. *Handbook of American Indians North of Mexico.* Totowa, N. J.: Rowman and Littlefield, 1960.

O'Meara, Walter. *Daughters of the Country: The Women of the Fur Traders and Mountain Men.* New York: Harcourt Brace Jovanovich, 1968.

Seaver, James E. *A Narrative of the Life of Mrs. Mary Jemison.* Gloucester, Mass.: Peter Smith, 1961.

THE AMERICAN REVOLUTION

Blumenthal, Walter Hart. *Women Camp Followers of the American Revolution.* New York: Arno, 1974.
De Pauw, Linda Grant. *Women of New York During the American Revolution.* Albany: New York State Bicentennial Commission, 1974.
Ellett, Elizabeth L. F. *The Women of the American Revolution.* New York: Haskell House, 1969.
Evans, Elizabeth. *Weathering the Storm: Women of the American Revolution.* New York: Charles Scribner's Sons, 1975.
Green, Harry and Mary W. *Pioneer Mothers of America.* New York: 1912.
Harkness, David J. *Southern Heroines of the American Revolution.* Knoxville, Tenn.: University of Tennessee Press, 1973.
Mann, Herman. *The Female Review: Life of Deborah Sampson.* New York: Arno, 1972.
Smith, Samuel Steele. *A Molly Pitcher Chronology.* Monmouth Beach, N. J.: Phillips Freneau, 1972.
Somerville, Mollie. *Women and the American Revolution.* Washington, D. C.: National Society of the Daughters of the American Revolution, 1974.
Thane, Elswyth. *Washington's Lady.* New York: Popular Library, 1972.

LOYALIST WOMEN

Brown, Marvin L., ed. *Baroness Von Riedesel and the American Revolution: Journal and Correspondence of a Tour of Duty.* Chapel Hill, N. C.: University of North Carolina Press, 1965.
Brown, Wallace. *The Good Americans.* New York: William Morrow, 1969.
Crary, Catherine C. *The Price of Loyalty.* New York: McGraw-Hill, 1973.
Flexner, James Thomas. *The Benedict Arnold Case.* New York: Collier-Macmillan, 1962.
Galloway, Grace Growden. *Diary of Grace Growden Galloway.* Reprinted. New York: Arno, 1971.
Tharp, Louise Hall. *The Baroness and the General.* Boston: Little, Brown, 1962.

Index